Betty Barkley
Bob Barkley

BLACK HILLS *treasures*

Favorite Recipes from the Black Forest Inn

Bob & Betty Barkley

BLACK HILLS treasures

Favorite Recipes from the Black Forest Inn

Bob & Betty Barkley

BLACK HILLS TREASURES

Favorite Recipes from the Black Forest Inn
Copyright © 2002 Bob and Betty Barkley
23191 Highway 385
Rapid City, South Dakota 57702
605-574-2000
www.blackforestinn.net

ISBN: 0-9713853-0-0

Edited, designed, and manufactured by
Favorite Recipes® Press, *an imprint of*

FRP

2451 Atrium Way
Nashville, Tennessee 37214
1-800-358-0560
Manufactured in the United States of America
First Printing: 2002   10,000 copies

Book Design: Starletta Polster
Art Director: Steve Newman
Managing Editor: Mary Cummings
Project Editor: Judy Jackson

Front cover photograph © 1996 Johnny Sundby

DEDICATION

In loving gratitude and with fond memories to my mother,

who allowed and encouraged me to experiment

in the kitchen from a very early age, and to my mother-in-law,

who convinced me and taught me that if you could cook for two,

you could cook for a crowd. Both women were models of

hospitality and generosity of spirit, and they had a love of sharing

food and fun in the kitchen and around the dining room table.

BLACK FOREST INN

Guests at the Black Forest Inn, situated in the heart of the Black Hills, often ask about its history. Originally, it was a restaurant with a reputation for good food and fun, under the direction of owner Bernice Musekamp. Bernice came to South Dakota in 1914, carrying a pet pigeon, little more than the clothes on her back, and a determination to live life to the hilt.

She once said, "My father bought a ranch in eastern South Dakota, and I got my first job cooking there. I didn't even know about boiling water, so I cooked twenty-four hours in advance. What I spoiled, I threw to the chickens. Chickens are crazy for burned beans."

Bernice bought a small ranch in the valley that is now Pactola Lake. She entered the restaurant business by picking wild raspberries to put on her angel food cake, which was smothered with thick, rich cream from her Jersey cow.

When the valley was acquired to become the Pactola Dam reservoir, Bernice moved to Musekamp Lodge, now known as the Black Forest Inn. Built in 1953, the Lodge lay nestled among the pines. The first meal served there, prepared by Bernice on her wood-burning cookstove, was Easter Sunday, 1954. The lodge was an instant success; specialties included fried chicken, corn on the cob, mashed potatoes, biscuits, salads, and cake or pie. Ordinary folks and dignitaries alike came in droves.

In the 1980s the Black Forest Inn was converted to a bed-and-breakfast. We have tried to continue the hospitality first exhibited by Bernice Musekamp and have added our own special touches. Each of the ten graciously appointed guest rooms has a private bath, antiques, handmade quilts, and a resident stuffed bear to welcome each guest. We want our guests to relax and enjoy the peace and serenity of the setting. Our motto is "where you are treated as a guest, but feel at home."

In addition to comfortable accommodations, delicious breakfasts made from scratch each morning are one of our specialties. A recent returning guest was overheard to say, "The bed is good, but I come for the breakfast." Since guests often request recipes for the delicious foods they have enjoyed, we have compiled this collection of favorite recipes, *Black Hills Treasures.* The history of the Black Forest Inn and its reputation for good food continues.

Bob Barkley Betty Barkley

TABLE OF contents

APPETIZERS, SALADS AND beverages

MOUNT RUSHMORE

FEW ATTRACTIONS STIR THE EMOTIONS of visitors the way Mount Rushmore does. Since its completion in 1941, it has joined the Statue of Liberty and the Stars-and-Stripes as one of America's most inspiring symbols of democracy. Each year, the 2.7 million visitors who come to gaze at the colossal faces of Presidents Washington, Jefferson, Roosevelt, and Lincoln go away enriched for having been here.

The awesome and impressive granite faces of the four American presidents tower 5,500 feet above sea level and are scaled to men who would stand 465 feet tall. Gutzon Borglum, who sculpted Mount Rushmore, said, "A monument's dimensions should be determined by the importance to civilization of the events commemorated....Let us place there, carved high, as close to heaven as we can, the words of our leaders, their faces, to show posterity what manner of men they were. Then breathe a prayer that these records will endure until the wind and the rain alone shall wear them away."

As he so brilliantly planned, their faces appear mobile and fluid when they catch both the morning and the afternoon sun. The likenesses are incredible. It's art, on a grand scale. And then the message of the memorial sinks in, and many are so moved that they experience a rekindled pride in our nation and its freedoms. This ambitious sculpture has become one of the nation's most beloved national memorials, symbolizing this country's unflinching dedication to freedom and democracy.

Photo by South Dakota Tourism

APPETIZERS, SALADS AND BEVERAGES

CHEESE BALLS

1	cup shredded sharp Cheddar cheese	4	teaspoons dry onion soup mix
1/2	cup all-purpose flour	1/4	teaspoon cayenne pepper
1/2	cup self-rising flour	6	tablespoons margarine

Mix the cheese, all-purpose flour, self-rising flour, soup mix and cayenne pepper in a bowl. Cut in the margarine with a pastry blender, mixing until it holds together. Shape by teaspoonfuls into balls. Place on an ungreased baking sheet. Bake at 350 degrees for 20 to 25 minutes or until golden brown. Cool on a wire rack. Serve immediately or freeze for future use.

Note: This amount of cayenne pepper is fairly mild. You might want to start with this and increase it if this is too tame for you.

Makes about 3 dozen

CREAM CHEESE CHUTNEY SPREAD

1   (8-ounce) block cream cheese,
     slightly softened
1/2 cup Earl Grey chutney or
     other chutney

1   teaspoon Pickapeppa Sauce,
     or to taste

Place the cream cheese on a serving dish. Spread the chutney over the cream cheese, allowing it to run down the sides. Sprinkle with Pickapeppa Sauce. Spread gently with a knife. Serve with crackers.

Note: Pickapeppa Sauce can be found in the condiment section of most supermarkets.

Serves 8 to 10

GARDEN FRESH SALSA

This salsa is great with fresh tomatoes, but in the winter, when tomatoes are tasteless and expensive, I use canned ones.

3	or 4 ripe tomatoes, chopped	2	(or more) jalapeño chiles,
1/4	cup chopped onion		finely chopped
1/4	cup coarsely chopped fresh		Juice of 1 lime
	cilantro		Salt to taste

Combine the tomatoes, onion, cilantro, jalapeños and lime juice in a bowl and mix well. Season with salt. Serve with tortilla chips. Store any leftovers in the refrigerator.

Note: Both the seeds and membranes of jalapeños can burn, so wear rubber gloves when handling them and be careful not to touch your eyes.

Makes about 1 cup

CHEESE PUFFS

These appetizers can be made ahead and stored in the freezer for up to a month. They are a great entertaining secret because you can be ready for guests with something hot from the oven in less than 15 minutes.

1	pound sharp Cheddar cheese, shredded	1	loaf hearty bread, cut into 1- to 1½-inch cubes
1	cup (2 sticks) butter, very soft		Dash of cayenne pepper

Combine the cheese and butter in a bowl. Spread over one side of each bread cube. It is not necessary to spread on all sides, because when the cheese melts it will cover the bread. Freeze on a baking sheet. When frozen, place in a freezer bag and store until ready to bake. Bake at 450 degrees for 5 to 7 minutes. Serve hot. May be baked immediately instead of freezing.

Serves 8 to 10

WINE BISCUITS

These slightly sweet, peppery biscuits taste great with a glass of wine. The unique combination of flavors will delight your taste buds.

1	cup all-purpose flour	3/4	teaspoon cracked pepper
2¹/2	tablespoons sugar	1/4	cup vegetable oil
1/2	teaspoon baking powder	1/4	cup red wine
1/4	teaspoon salt		

Combine the flour, sugar, baking powder, salt and pepper in a medium bowl. Mix the vegetable oil and wine in a small bowl. Add to the flour mixture, stirring just until moistened. Shape into a 1-inch diameter log. Cut into 1/4-inch slices. Place on an ungreased baking sheet.

Bake at 350 degrees for 12 minutes. Turn with a small turner. Bake for 6 minutes or until lightly browned. Cool on a wire rack. Store in an airtight container.

Makes 2 to 2¹/2 dozen

STUFFED MUSHROOMS

18   *large mushrooms*
2   *tablespoons chopped onion*
1/4 *cup (1/2 stick) butter*
1   *cup stuffing mix*
1   *cup chicken broth*

1/4 *cup finely chopped parsley*
2   *tablespoons lemon juice*
1/2 *teaspoon salt*
1   *(6-ounce) can crab meat,*
     flaked

Clean the mushrooms thoroughly. Snap off and chop the stems. Sauté the mushroom stems and onion in the butter in a skillet until tender. Remove from the heat. Combine the stuffing mix, chicken broth, parsley, lemon juice, salt and sautéed vegetables in a medium bowl and mix well. Stir in the crab meat.

Spoon the crab meat mixture into the mushroom caps. Place in a shallow baking pan sprayed with nonstick cooking spray. Bake at 375 degrees for 20 minutes or until heated through. Serve hot.

Makes 18

CRAB MEAT PIZZA

Not really a pizza, of course, but shaped and topped like one.

12	ounces cream cheese, softened	1	tablespoon minced dried onion
2	tablespoons Worcestershire sauce	1/2	teaspoon garlic salt
1	tablespoon lemon juice	1/2	(12-ounce) bottle chili sauce
2	tablespoons mayonnaise	1	(6-ounce) can crab meat, flaked
		2	tablespoons chopped parsley

Mix the cream cheese, Worcestershire sauce, lemon juice, mayonnaise, onion and garlic salt in a bowl. Spread in a circle on a round serving platter. Chill, covered, until serving time. Spread the chili sauce over the cream cheese mixture. Top with the crab meat and sprinkle with the parsley. Serve with rich buttery crackers.

Note: This can be prepared a day or two ahead and topped the day of serving. A large deep platter or plate works best.

Serves 12 to 15

COCKTAIL MEATBALLS AND FRANKS

1   *pound ground beef*
1   *egg, beaten*
1/4 *cup dry bread crumbs*
1/4 *cup finely chopped onion*
1/2 *teaspoon salt*
3/4 *cup chili sauce*

1/4 *cup grape jelly*
   Juice of 1/2 lemon (about 2
   tablespoons)
2/3 *cup water*
1   *pound fully cooked cocktail*
   franks

Combine the ground beef, egg, bread crumbs, onion and salt in a medium bowl and mix well. Shape into small balls. Combine the chili sauce, jelly, lemon juice and water in a large skillet and bring to a boil. Add the meatballs. Simmer until the ground beef is cooked through. Add the cocktail franks and simmer until heated through. Serve with cocktail picks.

Note: This dish can be prepared ahead up to the addition of the franks. Store, covered, in the refrigerator. Reheat the meatballs first; then add the franks and simmer until heated through.

Serves 14 to 16

FRUIT SALAD WITH GINGER AND LIME

1/4	*cup sugar*	*3*	*kiwifruit, peeled and sliced*
2	*tablespoons minced crystallized ginger*	*2*	*pints strawberries, rinsed, hulled and cut into quarters*
1/2	*cup fresh lime juice*	*1*	*small pineapple, peeled and cut into chunks*
1	*mango, peeled and cubed*		

For the dressing, stir the sugar and ginger into the lime juice in a bowl. Let stand to allow the flavors to blend. Combine the mango, kiwifruit, strawberries and pineapple in a serving bowl. Add the dressing and toss gently to coat. Chill, covered, in the refrigerator for several hours to overnight. Stir gently before serving.

Serves 6

SPINACH WALNUT SALAD

¹/₂ cup olive oil	*¹/₂ cup thinly sliced red onion*
¹/₄ cup rice vinegar	*¹/₂ cup chopped celery*
¹/₄ cup ketchup	*1 cup bean sprouts*
¹/₄ cup honey	*¹/₂ cup chopped walnuts, toasted*
¹/₂ teaspoon salt	*2 hard-boiled eggs, sliced*
2 bunches spinach, rinsed and torn into pieces	

For the dressing, whisk the olive oil, vinegar, ketchup, honey and salt in a bowl. Combine the spinach, onion, celery, bean sprouts, walnuts and eggs in a salad bowl. Add the dressing and toss lightly. Serve immediately.

Serves 8

SPINACH AND FRUIT WITH RASPBERRY DRESSING

1	bunch fresh spinach, rinsed and trimmed	1	mango, peeled and cubed
1/2	pint fresh strawberries, rinsed, hulled and cut into halves	1	kiwifruit, peeled and sliced
		1/2	cup chopped pecans
			Raspberry Dressing (below)

Combine the spinach, strawberries, mango, kiwifruit and pecans in a large salad bowl. Pour Raspberry Dressing over the top and toss to mix well. Serve immediately.

Serves 6 to 8

RASPBERRY DRESSING

1/4	cup raspberry wine vinegar	1/8	teaspoon salt, or to taste
1/4	cup sugar	1/8	teaspoon red pepper flakes
2	shallots, cut into quarters	1/4	cup vegetable oil

Process the vinegar, sugar, shallots, salt and red pepper flakes in a blender until the shallots are puréed. With the blender running at low speed, add the vegetable oil in a steady stream. Process until mixed well.

Makes about 1 cup

AUNT DORA'S SALAD

Most of us probably don't make as many gelatin salads as our mothers and grandmothers did. I think it was probably a necessity that they have ingredients on hand for a quick salad, when they couldn't run to the market as we can now. This salad was a must at every Barkley family dinner. Aunt Dora was a wonderful cook and a precious lady, and I submit this recipe in her memory.

1	small package lemon gelatin	1/2	cup sugar
3/4	cup boiling water	2	tablespoons all-purpose flour
1	(15-ounce) can crushed pineapple	1/2	teaspoon salt
2	bananas, sliced	1	egg, beaten
1	cup miniature marshmallows	1	cup whipped topping
		1	cup shredded Cheddar cheese

Dissolve the gelatin in the boiling water in a bowl. Drain the pineapple, reserving the juice. Add the pineapple and bananas to the gelatin mixture. Stir in the marshmallows. Pour into a shallow 2-quart serving dish. Chill until almost set. Combine the reserved pineapple juice, sugar, flour, salt and egg in a small saucepan. Cook over medium heat until thickened, stirring frequently. Remove from the heat and let cool. Fold in the whipped topping. Spread over the gelatin. Sprinkle with the cheese. Chill until serving time.

Serves 6 to 8

SPRING GREENS WITH HONEY MUSTARD DRESSING

8   ounces spring greens or lettuce
1   carrot, shredded
1   pint grape tomatoes

1   jicama, peeled and julienned
    Honey Mustard Dressing
    (below)

Arrange the greens on individual salad plates. Top each with some of the carrot, tomatoes and jicama. Spoon Honey Mustard Dressing over each salad.

Note: A root vegetable sometimes called a Mexican potato, jicama can be purchased in most supermarkets. It has a sweet, nutty taste and a texture like water chestnuts.

Serves 6

HONEY MUSTARD DRESSING

3/4   cup mayonnaise or light
      mayonnaise
1/4   cup honey

2   teaspoons Worcestershire sauce
3   tablespoons spicy brown mustard
2   teaspoons lemon juice

Whisk the mayonnaise, honey, Worcestershire sauce, mustard and lemon juice in a bowl. Pour into a jar with a tight-fitting lid. Store in the refrigerator. Shake well before using.

Makes 1 cup

PARMESAN BASIL PASTA SALAD

2   to 3 garlic cloves, minced
3   tablespoons lemon juice
3   tablespoons rice vinegar
1/2 teaspoon salt
1/4 teaspoon freshly ground pepper
1/3 cup olive oil
3   cups cooked penne pasta
3/4 cup grated Parmesan cheese

1/2 cup chopped fresh basil
1/2 cup black olives, whole or cut
    into halves
1   pint cherry tomatoes or grape
    tomatoes, cut into halves
1   carrot, peeled and shredded
2   cups chopped cooked chicken
    breast (optional)

For the dressing, combine the garlic, lemon juice, vinegar, salt, pepper and olive oil in a bowl and whisk until mixed. Combine the pasta, cheese, basil, olives, tomatoes, carrot and chicken in a large salad bowl. Pour the dressing over the salad and toss well. Serve immediately or chill, covered, in the refrigerator until serving time.

Serves 4

WILD RICE ORANGE SALAD

This salad is excellent as it is, but it is also delicious with the addition of cooked chicken.

2 cups cooked wild rice	1/4 cup orange juice
3/4 cup golden raisins	1 tablespoon balsamic vinegar
1/2 cup chopped pecans	2 teaspoons sugar
1/2 cup sliced celery	1 teaspoon grated orange zest
1/4 cup olive oil	Lettuce leaves

Combine the rice, raisins, pecans and celery in a large salad bowl. Whisk the olive oil, orange juice, vinegar, sugar and orange zest in a bowl. Pour over the rice mixture and toss to coat. Chill, covered, in the refrigerator overnight. Bring to room temperature before serving. If adding chicken, serve cold. Serve on lettuce leaves.

Serves 4

HOT SPICED TEA

Guests at our holiday open house have really enjoyed this.

1	quart boiling water	3	tea bags
1/3	cup sugar	1 1/2	cups orange juice
1	cinnamon stick	1	tablespoon lemon juice
1	teaspoon whole cloves	1/2	teaspoon grated orange zest

Combine the boiling water, sugar, cinnamon stick and cloves in a medium saucepan. Bring to a full rolling boil. Remove from the heat and add the tea bags. Steep for 4 minutes. Strain through a sieve. Stir in the orange juice, lemon juice and orange zest. Serve hot.

Serves 4

PEACH TEA

This is a wonderful, refreshing drink, but I might not have considered including the recipe in the cookbook because it is so easy to make I hardly consider it a recipe. However, so many guests have requested the recipe that I decided to include it.

2	cups boiling water	4	cups cranapple juice
2	peach-flavored tea bags		Ice
2	to 3 tablespoons sugar or artificial sweetener, or to taste		Sprigs of fresh mint (optional)

Pour the boiling water over the tea bags in a large bowl and steep for 5 minutes. Remove and discard the tea bags. Stir the sugar and cranapple juice into the tea. Let stand to cool. Pour into a serving pitcher filled with ice. Serve in chilled glasses. Add a sprig of mint to each glass.

Makes 6 cups

SUMMER MINT DRINK

1	cup sugar	1/2	cup orange juice concentrate
2	cups water	2/3	cup lemon juice
1	cup mint leaves		7-Up or water

To prepare the mint concentrate, bring the sugar and water to a boil in a medium saucepan. Remove from the heat and add the mint leaves. Let steep for 1 hour. Remove and discard the mint leaves. Add the orange juice concentrate and lemon juice and mix well. Cover and store in the refrigerator.

To serve, pour 1/3 cup mint concentrate into a tall glass. Fill with 7-Up or water and stir to mix. Add ice.

Makes about 3 cups concentrate

BREAKFAST AND breads

THE BLACK HILLS OF SOUTH DAKOTA

INTIMATE IS THE WORD OFTEN USED TO DESCRIBE the Black Hills. They invite you to hike, explore, and experience these friendly mountains. Eighteen peaks exceed 7,000 feet, and you can climb to the summit of every one of them. The Black Hills gorges and canyons are spectacular, yet very accessible. The Hills are an island of mountains in a sea of prairies and rangelands. They cover an area the size of Delaware, about 6,000 square miles.

Among the many gorgeous drives in the Black Hills, two have gained National Scenic Byways status. These roads are famous for their ability to transform an ordinary driving experience into a sightseeing adventure of wilderness, wildlife, and waterfalls. The seventy-mile Peter Norbeck Scenic Byway has been named one of the ten Most Outstanding Byways in America. This oval-shaped route winds through the most rugged real estate in the Black Hills. The Byway includes picturesque lakes, towering granite formations, six picture-perfect tunnels, tight hairpin curves, spiral "pigtail" bridges, and the wildlife ranges of Norbeck Wildlife Preserve, Black Elk National Wilderness Area, and Custer State Park. Spearfish Canyon showcases thousand-foot-high limestone palisades towering on each side of Highway 14A as it twists through the nineteen-mile gorge. Spearfish Creek lines the canyon floor, while canyon waterfalls make for popular roadside attractions. The list of claims to fame continues. But the fact is, the Black Hills enjoy an impressive blend of natural and man-made features for your family to explore, with beauty and diversity few places on this continent can offer.

Overleaf: Pactola Lake

BREAKFAST AND BREADS

SAVORY BAKED EGGS

1   pound lean bulk sausage
12 eggs
1/3 cup all-purpose flour
3/4 teaspoon baking powder
12 ounces cottage cheese

4   cups shredded Monterey Jack
    cheese
2   to 3 ounces garlic and herb-
    flavored feta cheese, crumbled

Brown the sausage in a skillet, stirring until crumbly; drain well. Beat the eggs in a bowl. Add the flour and baking powder and whisk to mix. Add the sausage, cottage cheese, Monterey Jack cheese and feta cheese. Spoon into a 9x13-inch baking pan sprayed with nonstick cooking spray. Bake at 350 degrees for 30 to 35 minutes or until a knife inserted near the center comes out clean.

Note: This dish can be made a day ahead. Cover and store in the refrigerator overnight; then bake as directed the next day. Increase the baking time by 5 to 10 minutes. Sometimes I brown several pounds of sausage at a time and freeze each pound in a separate freezer bag. The sausage keeps well for 4 to 6 weeks.

Serves 10

DENVER BAKE

2	tablespoons butter or olive oil	1/4	teaspoon pepper
1/2	cup chopped onion	8	cups hearty French or Italian
1	cup julienned mixed red and		bread cubes
	green bell peppers	1 1/2	cups cubed ham
1	tablespoon minced garlic	2	cups shredded sharp Cheddar
8	eggs		cheese
3	cups half-and-half	1/2	cup grated Parmesan cheese
1	teaspoon salt		

Heat the butter in a large sauté pan over medium heat. Add the onion and bell peppers and sauté for 5 to 8 minutes or until tender. Add the garlic and sauté for 1 minute. Remove from the heat and set aside.

Whisk the eggs, half-and-half, salt and pepper in a bowl. Add the bread cubes, sautéed vegetables, ham, Cheddar cheese and half the Parmesan cheese and mix well. Spoon into a buttered 9x13-inch baking pan. Sprinkle with the remaining Parmesan cheese. Let stand for 15 minutes for the bread to absorb the liquid or cover and chill in the refrigerator overnight. Bake at 350 degrees for 45 to 50 minutes or until the top is puffy and a knife inserted near the center comes out clean. If refrigerated, increase baking time by about 10 minutes.

Serves 8 to 10

HASH BROWN OVEN OMELET

This is very easy and very good. I crush the onion soup mix by rolling the unopened package with a rolling pin. This small amount of soup mix is not overwhelming but does give a great flavor. The preparation time is about 10 to 15 minutes for the first step, 5 minutes for the second.

1¼	pounds frozen hash browns, thawed	1	pound shredded Cheddar, pepper Jack or Monterey Jack cheese, or a combination
2	cups cubed ham		
1	teaspoon onion soup mix, crushed	8	large eggs
		¼	cup half-and-half
2	tablespoons butter, melted		Chopped parsley (optional)

Using paper towels, squeeze as much moisture as possible from the hash browns. Press into a 9x13-inch baking pan sprayed with nonstick cooking spray. Sprinkle with the ham and soup mix. Drizzle with the butter. Spread half the cheese over the top. Chill, covered, in the refrigerator overnight.

Uncover the hash browns and bake at 375 degrees for 15 minutes. Beat the eggs and half-and-half in a bowl. Reduce the oven temperature to 350 degrees. Remove the hash browns from the oven and pour the egg mixture over the top. Top with the remaining cheese. Bake for 15 to 20 minutes or until the eggs are done. Sprinkle with parsley.

Serves 8 to 10

CHILE CHEESE SQUARES

6   eggs
1/4   cup all-purpose flour
1/2   teaspoon baking powder
1/8   teaspoon salt
1/8   teaspoon cayenne pepper
2   tablespoons butter, melted

2   cups shredded Monterey Jack cheese
1   cup cottage cheese
1   (4-ounce) can chopped green chiles

Whisk the eggs in a large bowl. Stir in the flour, baking powder, salt, cayenne pepper and butter. Add the Monterey Jack cheese, cottage cheese and green chiles and mix well. Spoon into a 9x9-inch baking pan sprayed with nonstick cooking spray. Bake at 400 degrees for 10 minutes. Reduce the oven temperature to 350 degrees. Bake for 20 to 25 minutes or until the top is golden brown and a knife inserted near the center comes out clean. Let cool for several minutes before cutting into squares.

Serves 6

This is equally good as a breakfast dish or as an appetizer (cut it into 36 small squares for appetizers). For breakfast, we sometimes serve it with sour cream and salsa. It can be made ahead and stored, covered, in the refrigerator for up to 2 days. Reheat in the microwave or oven.

CRUSTLESS QUICHE

This egg dish takes a bit more preparation time, but its delicate texture and rich flavor make it worth the effort.

1/4 cup (1/2 stick) butter	1 cup cottage cheese
1/3 cup all-purpose flour	1 teaspoon baking powder
6 large eggs	1 teaspoon sugar
1 pound Monterey Jack, pepper Jack or sharp Cheddar cheese, or a combination, shredded	Freshly cracked pepper to taste
8 ounces cream cheese, softened	1 cup evaporated milk or whole milk

Melt the butter in a saucepan. Stir in the flour. Cook for 2 minutes, stirring until smooth. Set aside to cool. Beat the eggs in a large bowl with a whisk. Add the Monterey Jack cheese, cream cheese, cottage cheese, baking powder, sugar, pepper and cooled flour mixture and mix well. Stir in the evaporated milk. Spoon into individual quiche pans sprayed with nonstick cooking spray. Bake at 350 degrees for 30 to 35 minutes or until a knife inserted near the center comes out clean. Serve immediately.

Note: This quiche can also be prepared in a 9x13-inch baking pan. Increase the baking time to 40 to 45 minutes.

Serves 10

BOB'S POTATOES

8   to 10 slices lean bacon, chopped
1/4 cup vegetable oil
3   tablespoons butter
1   (2-pound) package frozen
     hash browns

Salt and pepper to taste
6   to 8 ounces sharp Cheddar
     cheese, shredded

Cook the bacon in a skillet until crisp; drain well and set aside. Heat the vegetable oil and butter in the skillet. (It should be hot enough to sizzle when you add the potatoes.) Add the potatoes. Cook, covered, until the potatoes are somewhat tender, stirring frequently. Add the bacon, salt and pepper. Cook until the potatoes are tender. Reduce the heat to low. Sprinkle with the cheese. Do not stir after adding the cheese. Serve portions directly from the skillet.

Serves 8 to 10

These potatoes are simple to prepare, but our guests rave about them! Since this recipe has been mentioned in some of our printed material and on our Web site, newly arrived guests ask, "Are we having Bob's potatoes for breakfast?"

BREAKFAST POTATOES

1/2 cup chopped onion	1 (2-pound) package frozen hash browns
1/4 cup (1/2 stick) butter	
8 ounces sharp Cheddar cheese, shredded	1 1/2 cups coarsely crushed cornflakes
2 cups sour cream	2 tablespoons butter, melted
1 (10-ounce) can cream of chicken soup	

Sauté the onion in 1/4 cup butter in a skillet until tender. Combine the sautéed onion, cheese, sour cream and undiluted soup in a bowl. Stir in the potatoes. Spoon into a 9x13-inch baking pan sprayed with nonstick cooking spray. Sprinkle a mixture of the cornflakes and 2 tablespoons butter over the top. Bake at 350 degrees for 40 to 50 minutes or until the potatoes are tender. This dish can be prepared ahead, refrigerated overnight, and baked the next day. It is wonderful for dinner, also.

Serves 10 to 12

BLACK FOREST INN GRANOLA

5 cups rolled oats	1 cup unsalted sunflower seeds
1/2 cup wheat germ	1/2 cup peanut butter
1/2 cup flaked coconut	1/2 cup honey or molasses
1/2 cup chopped walnuts or other nuts	1 teaspoon cinnamon

Combine the oats, wheat germ, coconut, walnuts and sunflower seeds in a large bowl
and mix well. Combine the peanut butter, honey and cinnamon in a microwave-safe bowl.
Microwave until warm. Add to the wheat germ mixture and mix well. Spread evenly on
2 baking sheets sprayed with nonstick cooking spray. Bake at 350 degrees until lightly
browned, stirring occasionally. Let stand until cool. Store in an airtight container.

Makes about 8 cups

BLACK FOREST INN FRENCH TOAST

1	loaf French or Italian bread	1/2	teaspoon cinnamon
2	eggs	1	tablespoon vanilla extract
1/2	cup half-and-half or	2	tablespoons margarine, melted
	evaporated milk	2	tablespoons vegetable oil
1/3	cup sugar	2	tablespoons butter

Cut the bread into 10 to 12 thick slices. Beat the eggs in a small shallow bowl. Add the half-and-half, sugar, cinnamon and vanilla. Stir in the melted margarine.

Heat the vegetable oil and butter to 350 degrees in an electric skillet. Dip the bread slices in the egg mixture. Cook until golden brown on both sides, turning once. Drain on paper towels on a warm baking sheet. Sprinkle with confectioners' sugar. Garnish with orange slices and strawberries. Bob's Potatoes (page 39) go well with this French toast.

Serves 6 to 8

STUFFED FRENCH TOAST

4	ounces cream cheese, softened	2	teaspoons vanilla extract
1/2	cup apricot preserves	1/4	teaspoon salt
1	loaf dry Italian or French bread	2	cups coarsely crushed
3	eggs		cornflakes
1/2	cup buttermilk	2	tablespoons butter
2	tablespoons sugar	2	tablespoons vegetable oil

Mix the cream cheese and apricot preserves in a bowl. Cut the bread into 3/8-inch slices. Make sandwiches using the cream cheese mixture. Mix the eggs, buttermilk, sugar, vanilla and salt in a bowl. Dip the sandwiches into the egg mixture, then into the cornflakes.

Heat the butter and vegetable oil to 350 degrees in an electric skillet. Fry the sandwiches until golden brown on both sides, turning once. Drain on paper towel-lined baking sheets. Serve immediately or hold in a warm oven until serving time.

Makes 7 to 8 sandwiches

CORNMEAL PANCAKES

3/4 cup all-purpose flour
2/3 cup cornmeal
1/3 cup sugar
1/4 teaspoon salt
3/4 teaspoon baking powder

1/4 teaspoon baking soda
3/4 cup buttermilk
1/4 cup milk
1 egg, beaten
2 tablespoons butter, melted

Mix the flour, cornmeal, sugar, salt, baking powder and baking soda in a medium bowl. Mix the buttermilk, milk, egg and butter in a small bowl. Add to the flour mixture all at once; whisk just until mixed.

Heat a nonstick griddle or electric skillet to 350 degrees. (A drop of water splashed on the griddle should sizzle.) Spoon the batter by 1/4 cupfuls onto the hot griddle, allowing room for the batter to spread. Cook for 2 to 3 minutes or until the bottom of the pancake is browned and the top begins to bubble. Flip with a thin spatula and cook for 1 to 2 minutes or until browned. Serve hot with your favorite butter and syrup.

Makes 10 to 12 pancakes

You can make excellent variations of these pancakes by sprinkling chopped nuts or fruit on the batter before you turn the pancakes.

POTATO PANCAKES

2	cups shredded potatoes	1	teaspoon minced fresh rosemary
1/4	cup milk	2	tablespoons grated Parmesan
2	eggs, beaten		cheese
2	tablespoons all-purpose flour	1/2	teaspoon salt
1	tablespoon grated onion, or	1/4	teaspoon pepper
	1/2 teaspoon onion powder	2	tablespoons (about) olive oil

Combine the uncooked potatoes, milk, eggs, flour, onion, rosemary, cheese, salt and pepper in a bowl and mix well. Heat the olive oil in a large heavy skillet over medium heat until a bit of the batter sizzles when dropped into the skillet. Spoon the batter by 1/4 cupfuls into the hot skillet. Cook until golden brown on the bottom. Turn the pancakes and cook until the other side is golden brown and the potatoes are tender. Drain on paper towels.

Makes 10 pancakes

We like to serve these with applesauce and bacon. They are also good with a bit of sour cream and parsley sprinkled on top.

PUMPKIN PANCAKES

2	cups all-purpose flour	1	cup canned pumpkin
2	tablespoons baking powder	1	(12-ounce) can evaporated milk
1/4	cup packed brown sugar	2	teaspoons vanilla extract
1	teaspoon salt	1/4	cup (1/2 stick) butter, melted
1	teaspoon cinnamon		and cooled slightly
1	teaspoon nutmeg	5	tablespoons butter, softened
1/2	teaspoon ground cloves	1/4	cup maple syrup
2	eggs		

Mix the flour, baking powder, brown sugar, salt, cinnamon, nutmeg and cloves in a
medium bowl. Beat the eggs in a large bowl. Add the pumpkin, evaporated milk, vanilla
and 1/4 cup butter and stir to combine. Add the flour mixture and stir to combine. Heat
a greased griddle over medium heat until drops of water dance on the surface. Drop
the batter by spoonfuls onto the hot griddle. Cook for 4 to 5 minutes or until golden
brown on both sides, turning once. (The batter may thicken as it stands; if so, add a
little milk. Any kind of milk will do; it need not be evaporated milk.)

For Maple Butter, combine 5 tablespoons butter and maple syrup in a bowl, stirring
until blended and smooth. Serve with the pancakes or with corn bread.

Makes about 20 pancakes

OVERNIGHT WHOLE WHEAT WAFFLES

1	envelope dry yeast	1	cup all-purpose flour
1/2	cup warm water	1	cup whole wheat flour
1	tablespoon sugar	1/4	teaspoon salt
2	cups milk	2	eggs, beaten
1/2	cup (1 stick) butter	1/4	teaspoon baking soda

Dissolve the yeast in the warm water in a large bowl. Stir in the sugar. Let stand for 5 to 10 minutes. Heat the milk and butter in a saucepan just until the butter is softened and can be incorporated into the milk. Cool to 110 degrees. Stir the milk mixture into the yeast mixture. Add the all-purpose flour, whole wheat flour and salt and whisk until mixed. Cover the bowl with plastic wrap topped with a towel. Let stand overnight at room temperature.

Add the eggs and baking soda to the batter and mix well. The batter will be thin. Pour onto a hot greased waffle iron. Bake until golden brown. Serve with fresh strawberries and whipped cream or your favorite syrup.

Note: This batter will keep for several days in the refrigerator. To prevent build-up on the waffle iron, brush it with vegetable oil rather than using nonstick cooking spray.

Makes about 5 waffles

RASPBERRY RHUBARB SAUCE

3   *cups chopped fresh or frozen rhubarb*
2   *tablespoons water*

1   *cup sugar*
3   *cups fresh raspberries*

Combine the rhubarb and water in a medium saucepan. Cook over medium heat until the rhubarb is tender, stirring frequently. Add the sugar. Simmer for 2 to 3 minutes. Add the raspberries. Cook for 3 to 4 minutes, stirring frequently. Serve warm over pancakes, crepes or waffles.

Makes about 3 cups

*If you use frozen raspberries in this recipe,
decrease the sugar by about 1/3 cup.*

APRICOT CREAM CHEESE COFFEE CAKE

*This recipe was originally created for a springform pan and was done in layers.
I thought that was too much work, and not everyone has a springform pan.
This is my much easier but just as good version.*

2¹/₂	cups all-purpose flour	³/₄	cup sour cream
1	cup sugar	2	eggs
³/₄	cup (1¹/₂ sticks) butter, softened	1	teaspoon vanilla extract
¹/₂	teaspoon baking powder	8	ounces cream cheese, softened
¹/₂	teaspoon baking soda	1	cup apricot preserves
¹/₄	teaspoon salt	¹/₂	cup chopped pecans

Combine the flour and sugar in a large mixer bowl. Add the butter. Beat at low speed
until mixed, scraping the bowl occasionally. Remove and reserve 1¹/₄ cups of this
mixture. Add the baking powder, baking soda, salt, sour cream, eggs, vanilla and cream
cheese to the remaining flour mixture and mix well. Spread in a greased 9x13-inch
baking pan. Spoon the preserves over the top. Sprinkle with the reserved flour mixture
and the pecans. Bake at 350 degrees for 30 to 35 minutes or until a wooden pick
inserted near the center comes out clean. Serve warm.

For Raspberry Almond Coffee Cake, substitute almond extract for the vanilla,
raspberry preserves for the apricot and sliced almonds for the pecans.

Serves 12 to 15

SOUR CREAM COFFEE CAKE

2¹/2 cups all-purpose flour
1 teaspoon baking soda
2 teaspoons baking powder
¹/4 teaspoon salt
³/4 cup (1¹/2 sticks) butter, softened
1¹/4 cups sugar
3 eggs

1¹/4 cups sour cream
1 teaspoon almond extract
¹/4 cup (¹/2 stick) butter, softened
¹/4 cup sugar
¹/3 cup all-purpose flour
1 teaspoon nutmeg
1 cup chopped pecans

Mix 2¹/2 cups flour, baking soda, baking powder and salt in a medium bowl. Cream
³/4 cup butter and 1¹/4 cups sugar in a mixer bowl until light and fluffy. Beat in the
eggs. Add the sour cream and almond extract. Add the flour mixture gradually, beating
well after each addition. Spoon into a greased 9x13-inch baking pan. Mix ¹/4 cup butter,
¹/4 cup sugar, ¹/3 cup flour, nutmeg and pecans in a bowl. Sprinkle over the batter. Bake
at 350 degrees for 30 to 35 minutes or until a wooden pick inserted near the center
comes out clean. Drizzle with Confectioners' Sugar Frosting (page 57) if desired. (Thin
the frosting with an additional 1 to 2 tablespoons milk.) Serve warm.

Makes 12 to 15 servings

BANANA NUT BREAD

This has been a favorite since the oat bran craze. I adapted a recipe by reducing the flour and adding the oat bran. I like to spread thin slices with a little butter and make "sandwiches" from it. Hopefully, the butter will not wipe out the benefits of the oat bran! I serve it with fruit for breakfast or with a salad for lunch.

1¹/₄	cups all-purpose flour	1	cup packed brown sugar
³/₄	cup oat bran	2	eggs
1	teaspoon baking soda	1	cup mashed very ripe bananas
¹/₂	teaspoon salt	2	teaspoons vanilla extract
¹/₂	cup (1 stick) margarine, softened	1	cup chopped walnuts

Mix the flour, oat bran, baking soda and salt in a medium bowl. Cream the margarine and brown sugar in a mixer bowl. Beat in the eggs. Add the bananas and mix well. Add the flour mixture and mix well. Stir in the vanilla and walnuts. Spoon into a greased and floured 5x9-inch loaf pan. Bake at 350 degrees for 45 to 55 minutes or until a wooden pick inserted near the center comes out clean. Cool in the pan on a wire rack for 15 minutes. Remove from the pan and cool completely. Store in a sealable plastic bag or wrapped in foil.

Makes 1 loaf

CRANBERRY PECAN BREAD

2	cups all-purpose flour	2/3	cup (about) buttermilk
1	cup sugar	1	egg, beaten
1/2	teaspoon salt	1/3	cup butter, melted
1	teaspoon baking powder	11/3	cups chopped cranberries
1/4	teaspoon baking soda	1/2	cup chopped pecans, toasted
	Grated zest and juice of	3	ounces cream cheese, softened
	1 large orange	1	tablespoon confectioners' sugar
2	tablespoons orange liqueur	2	tablespoons finely chopped
	(optional)		pecans, toasted

For the bread, mix the flour, sugar, salt, baking powder and baking soda in a large bowl. Mix the orange juice and liqueur in a measuring cup. Add enough buttermilk to measure 1 cup. Mix with the orange zest, egg and butter in a small bowl. Add to the flour mixture, stirring just until moistened. Fold in the cranberries and 1/2 cup pecans. Spoon into a greased 5x9-inch loaf pan. Bake at 375 degrees for 10 minutes. Reduce the oven temperature to 350 degrees. Bake for 45 minutes or until a wooden pick inserted near the center comes out clean. Cool in the pan for 15 minutes. Loosen carefully from the sides of the pan. Remove to a wire rack to cool completely. Wrap in foil. When ready to serve, slice thinly. For the filling, mix the cream cheese, confectioners' sugar and 2 tablespoons pecans in a bowl. Spread over half the bread slices. Assemble as "sandwiches."

Makes 1 loaf

POPPY SEED BREAD

2	cups all-purpose flour	1	teaspoon vanilla extract
1	teaspoon baking powder	1/2	cup poppy seeds
1	teaspoon salt	1	(12-ounce) can evaporated milk
2	eggs		Softened butter
1 1/2	cups sugar	1	tablespoon (about) sugar
3/4	cup vegetable oil		

Grease and flour two 4x8-inch or three 3x7-inch loaf pans. Mix the flour, baking powder and salt in a small bowl. Beat the eggs and 1 1/2 cups sugar in a mixer bowl until pale yellow. Add the vegetable oil and vanilla gradually. Stir in the poppy seeds. Add the flour mixture and evaporated milk alternately, beating well after each addition. The batter will be thin. Pour into the prepared loaf pans. Bake at 350 degrees until a wooden pick inserted near the center comes out clean, 45 to 55 minutes for the larger loaves, 35 to 40 minutes for the smaller loaves. Cool in the pans on a wire rack for 5 minutes. Brush the top of each loaf with softened butter and sprinkle with 1 tablespoon sugar. Cool in the pans for 15 minutes longer. Remove to a wire rack to cool completely. The flavor of these loaves is best the day after baking.

Makes 2 large or 3 small loaves

RHUBARB BREAD

2¹/₂ cups all-purpose flour
1   teaspoon baking soda
1   teaspoon salt
1¹/₂ cups packed brown sugar
²/₃ cup vegetable oil
1   egg
1   cup sour milk or buttermilk

2   teaspoons vanilla extract
1¹/₂ cups rhubarb, cut into ¹/₂-inch
     pieces
¹/₂ cup chopped walnuts
¹/₂ cup sugar
1   teaspoon cinnamon
2   tablespoons butter

Mix the flour, baking soda and salt in a bowl. Combine the brown sugar and vegetable oil in a large bowl. Stir in the egg, milk and vanilla. Add the flour mixture gradually, mixing after each addition. Stir in the rhubarb and walnuts. Spoon into 2 greased and floured 5x9-inch loaf pans. Sprinkle with a mixture of the sugar, cinnamon and butter. Bake at 350 degrees for 45 to 55 minutes or until a wooden pick inserted near the center comes out clean. Cool in the pans on a wire rack for 15 minutes. Loosen the loaves from the side of the pans. Remove to a wire rack to cool completely. Wrap in foil to store or place in sealable plastic bags.

Makes 2 loaves

PURPLE RIBBON ZUCCHINI BREAD

*Our son won a purple ribbon at the state fair when he was 10, so this is a
tried-and-true recipe—and maybe a little different from others you have tried. I like
to slice it thinly, spread it with a little butter and make sandwiches out of it to
serve with a salad in the summertime. It is also great sliced more
thickly and toasted for breakfast.*

3	cups all-purpose flour	1	cup vegetable oil
1	teaspoon salt	2	cups sugar
1	teaspoon baking soda	2	cups grated zucchini
1/4	teaspoon baking powder	1	tablespoon vanilla extract
1	tablespoon cinnamon	1/2	cup chopped walnuts
3	eggs, beaten	2	tablespoons sesame seeds

Mix the flour, salt, baking soda, baking powder and cinnamon in a medium bowl. Beat
the eggs, vegetable oil and sugar at medium speed in a mixer bowl until mixed well.
Stir in the zucchini and vanilla. Add the flour mixture gradually, stirring just until
mixed. Fold in the walnuts. Spoon into 2 greased and floured 5x9-inch loaf pans.
Sprinkle with the sesame seeds. Bake at 350 degrees for 50 to 60 minutes or until a
wooden pick inserted near the center comes out clean.

Makes 2 loaves

ROSEMARY SUN-DRIED TOMATO BREAD

1	envelope dry yeast	1	egg, beaten
1	cup warm (105 to 115 degrees) water	1/4	cup (1/2 stick) butter, melted and cooled
3	cups all-purpose flour	2	tablespoons drained chopped sun-dried tomatoes
1	teaspoon salt		
2	teaspoons dried minced onion, or 2 tablespoons minced fresh onion	1/2	cup grated Parmesan cheese
		1	tablespoon olive oil
			Coarse salt
1	tablespoon sugar		Chopped sun-dried tomatoes
1	teaspoon Italian seasoning		Chopped fresh rosemary
1	teaspoon minced fresh rosemary		

Dissolve the yeast in the warm water in a large bowl. Combine 2 cups of the flour and the next 5 ingredients in a bowl. Add to the yeast mixture. Add the egg, butter and 2 tablespoons sun-dried tomatoes. Stir in the remaining 1 cup flour and cheese. Let rise, covered, in a warm place until doubled in bulk. Stir down the dough. Knead for 1 to 2 minutes on a floured surface. Divide the dough into 2 portions. Shape each portion into a 1/2-inch-thick oval on a greased baking sheet. Brush the surface of the dough with the olive oil. Sprinkle with coarse salt and additional sun-dried tomatoes and rosemary. Let rise, covered, for 30 to 45 minutes or until doubled in bulk. Bake at 350 degrees for 25 to 30 minutes or until the loaves test done. Serve warm.

Makes 2 loaves

QUICK BREAKFAST ROLLS

1 cup all-purpose flour	1/2 cup apricot or peach preserves
1 cup whole wheat flour	3 ounces cream cheese, softened
4 teaspoons baking powder	1 tablespoon butter, softened
1/2 teaspoon salt	1 tablespoon milk
1/2 teaspoon cream of tartar	1 teaspoon almond extract
1/2 cup (1 stick) butter	1/8 teaspoon salt
1 teaspoon almond extract	1 cup confectioners' sugar
2/3 cup milk	

Mix the all-purpose flour, whole wheat flour, baking powder, 1/2 teaspoon salt and cream of tartar in a large bowl. Cut in 1/2 cup butter with a pastry blender until crumbly. Add 1 teaspoon almond extract and the milk to the flour mixture and mix well. Knead on a floured board for about 30 seconds. Roll into an 8x12-inch rectangle. Mix the apricot preserves and cream cheese in a bowl. Spread over the dough. Beginning on a long side, roll into a tight roll. Pinch the edges together. Cut into 1-inch pieces with a very sharp knife. Place cut side up on a baking sheet sprayed with nonstick cooking spray. Bake at 400 degrees for 15 minutes or until golden brown on top and bottom. Cool on the pan on a wire rack for 15 minutes. For Confectioners' Sugar Frosting, blend 1 tablespoon butter, 1 tablespoon milk, 1 teaspoon almond extract, 1/8 teaspoon salt and confectioners' sugar in a bowl. Spread over the rolls.

Serves 12

LIGHT YEAST ROLLS

1¹/4 cups milk
3   tablespoons sugar
1   envelope dry yeast
2³/4 cups all-purpose flour
³/4   cup whole wheat flour

1   teaspoon salt
1   large egg, lightly beaten
¹/2   cup (1 stick) unsalted butter,
        softened

Heat the milk and sugar in a saucepan until warm, stirring to dissolve the sugar. Sprinkle the yeast over the top. Let stand for 10 minutes. Stir in the egg. Combine the all-purpose flour, whole wheat flour and salt in a mixer bowl. Mix with dough hook. Add the milk mixture in a steady stream, beating constantly at low speed. Beat for 1 minute longer. Add the butter ¹/4 at a time with the mixer at low speed. Beat at medium speed for 2 minutes. Knead on a floured surface for 1 minute. Place in a greased large bowl, turning to coat the surface. Let stand, covered, in a warm place for 1 hour or until doubled in bulk. Punch down the dough. Let stand for 5 minutes. Knead the dough lightly on a floured surface. Shape into a cylinder about 30 inches long. Cut 1 end at a 45-degree angle. Cut the remaining dough into 24 triangles. Place on 2 parchment paper-lined baking sheets. Let stand for 30 minutes or until almost doubled in bulk. Bake at 375 degrees for 15 minutes or until golden brown. Cool slightly on the pans on a wire rack. Remove to a wire rack to cool completely. Serve warm.

Makes 2 dozen

RICH YEAST ROLLS

5½ cups all-purpose flour
¼ cup sugar
1 teaspoon salt
1 cup (2 sticks) margarine
2 envelopes dry yeast
½ cup warm (105 to 115 degrees) water

1 cup warm milk
2 eggs, beaten
2 to 3 tablespoons butter, softened
¼ cup sugar
1 teaspoon cinnamon
Confectioners' Sugar Frosting (page 57)

Combine the flour, ¼ cup sugar and salt in a large bowl. Cut in the margarine until crumbly. Sprinkle the yeast over the warm water, stirring until dissolved. Add the milk, eggs and yeast mixture to the flour mixture and mix well. Cover with plastic wrap, then a towel. Let stand for 20 minutes. Punch down the dough. Turn out on floured board.

Shape the dough into a 10x18-inch rectangle. Brush with butter. Sprinkle with ¼ cup sugar and cinnamon. Shape into an 18-inch-long roll. Pinch the edges to seal. Cut into 24 rolls. Place 1 inch apart in 9x13-inch baking pans. Cover with waxed paper sprayed with nonstick cooking spray, then with plastic wrap. Chill for 2 to 24 hours. Uncover the rolls and let stand at room temperature for 10 minutes. Bake at 350 degrees for 25 to 30 minutes or until golden brown. Cool in the pans on a wire rack for 15 minutes. Remove to a wire rack to cool completely. Spread with Confectioners' Sugar Frosting.

Makes 2 dozen

PARMESAN ROSEMARY POPOVERS

1 tablespoon (about) grated Parmesan cheese

2 cups milk

2 tablespoons butter, melted and cooled

2 cups all-purpose flour

1/2 teaspoon salt

1/2 teaspoon freshly cracked pepper

2 teaspoons minced fresh rosemary

1/4 cup grated Parmesan cheese

4 eggs

Have all ingredients at room temperature. Spray popover pans or large muffin cups with nonstick cooking spray. Sprinkle with 1 tablespoon Parmesan cheese. Combine the milk, butter, flour, salt, pepper, rosemary and 1/4 cup Parmesan cheese in a medium bowl and mix just until smooth. Stir in the eggs one at a time; do not overmix.

Fill the popover pans 3/4 full. Bake at 450 degrees for 15 minutes. Reduce the oven temperature to 350 degrees; do not open the oven. Bake for 20 minutes or until the sides are golden brown and firm. (Remove 1 popover to test for doneness.) Insert a sharp knife gently into each popover to allow steam to escape. Serve immediately.

Makes 8

SCONES

2¹/₄ cups bread flour
2¹/₄ cups cake flour
¹/₂ cup sugar
4 teaspoons baking powder
¹/₂ teaspoon salt
1 cup (2 sticks) butter
4 eggs

¹/₂ cup heavy cream
¹/₂ cup dried sweetened
  cranberries or currants
  (optional)
1 egg
1 tablespoon water

Sift the bread flour, cake flour, sugar, baking powder and salt into a bowl. Cut in the butter until crumbly. Beat 4 eggs and the cream in a mixer bowl. Add to the flour mixture and mix just until moistened; do not overmix. Fold in the cranberries. Divide the dough into halves. Pat each half into a 1/2-inch-thick circle on a floured surface. Cut each into 6 wedges. Place on a greased or parchment paper-lined baking sheet. Brush the tops of the scones with a mixture of 1 egg and water. Bake at 350 degrees for 15 to 20 minutes or until light golden brown. These scones freeze well.

Note: I use parchment paper because I would rather cook than wash dishes. Ask your supermarket bakery if they will sell you parchment sheets. I have found this to be the most economical source.

Makes 12

MAIN *dishes*

BADLANDS OF SOUTH DAKOTA

ALL THINGS CONSIDERED, THERE ARE A great many reasons for travelers to be lured to the Badlands National Park. The landscape of sharp ridges, steep-walled canyons, and deep gorges, which has been ruthlessly shaped by wind and water, is picturesque and, in its own way, beautiful. The unique topography has given a strange beauty to this almost desolate land, so much so that more than 160 square miles of it has been reserved for inclusion in our National Parks System. At the overlooks along the Badlands State Scenic Byway, the vistas of prairie grasses give way to a vast and jumbled wilderness.

However, the marvels of Badlands topography are not the region's only claim to fame. It is likely that representative samples of Great Plains wildlife can be enjoyed during your visit to the Park.

Eagles and turkey vultures ride the updrafts, while deer and antelope are usually visible in the upper grasslands. Wily coyotes will likely be seen hunting in the midst of one of the biggest prairie dog towns you have ever seen. In the basins you may spot some grazing bison.

Observe, study, and enjoy the silence of this magnificent and unique land. Whatever your impression of the Badlands may be, you will come away knowing you have experienced one of the rare treasures of this great nation.

MAIN DISHES

PRIME RIB

1	teaspoon minced fresh rosemary, or $^1/_2$ teaspoon dried rosemary	2	garlic cloves, minced
1	teaspoon minced fresh oregano, or $^1/_2$ teaspoon dried oregano	1	teaspoon (about) freshly ground pepper
1	teaspoon minced fresh thyme, or $^1/_2$ teaspoon dried thyme	1	teaspoon (about) coarse salt
		1	(3- to 4-pound) boneless prime rib
			Olive oil

Mix the rosemary, oregano, thyme, garlic, pepper and salt in a small bowl. Rub the beef with a small amount of olive oil. Rub with the seasoning mixture. Place the beef in a roaster. Bake at 500 degrees for 15 minutes. Reduce the oven temperature to 350 degrees; do not open the oven. Bake for 45 to 55 minutes for medium. Remove from the oven. Cover loosely with foil and let stand for 15 to 20 minutes. The beef will continue cooking during the standing time. Cut into $^3/_4$- to 1-inch slices.

Serves 4 to 6

GARLIC THYME FLANK STEAK

1½ pounds flank steak
2 tablespoons olive oil
½ teaspoon salt
¼ teaspoon pepper
1 cup beef broth
2 tablespoons coarsely chopped parsley
2 garlic cloves, minced

2 teaspoons minced fresh thyme, or ½ teaspoon dried thyme, crushed
⅓ cup sherry
Water
3 tablespoons cornstarch
½ cup cold water

Score the steak at 1-inch intervals. Heat the olive oil in an ovenproof skillet. Add the steak and cook over medium-high heat until browned. Season with salt and pepper. Mix the beef broth, parsley, garlic and thyme in a bowl. Pour over the steak. Bake, covered, at 325 degrees for 1½ to 2 hours or until the steak is tender. Remove the steak to a serving platter and keep warm.

For the gravy, measure the pan drippings. Add the sherry and enough water to measure 1¼ cups. Pour into the skillet. Stir in a mixture of the cornstarch and ½ cup water. Cook until the mixture is slightly thickened, stirring constantly. Pour a small amount over the steak. Serve the remaining gravy on the side. Garnish with additional parsley. Serve with garlic mashed potatoes.

Serves 4 to 6

MINUTE STEAK AND POTATO BAKE

1	cup sliced onion	1/4	teaspoon pepper
1	cup sliced mushrooms	1/4	teaspoon dry mustard
1/4	cup (1/2 stick) butter	2	cups buttermilk
4	cube steaks	2	tablespoons chopped parsley
1/4	cup all-purpose flour	4	cups sliced uncooked potatoes
1	teaspoon salt		

Sauté the onion and mushrooms in the butter in a skillet for 5 minutes or until tender. Remove the sautéed vegetables and set aside. Brown the steaks in the skillet. Remove and set aside.

Add the flour, salt, pepper and dry mustard to the pan drippings in the skillet, stirring until mixed. Remove from the heat. Stir in the buttermilk gradually. Cook until thickened, stirring constantly. Stir in the parsley.

Layer the potatoes, steaks and sautéed vegetables in a 9x13-inch baking dish sprayed with nonstick cooking spray. Pour the buttermilk mixture over the top. Bake, covered with foil, at 350 degrees for 1 1/4 hours. Garnish with sprigs of fresh parsley.

Serves 4

SWISS STEAK

6	(6-ounce) cube steaks	1/4	cup all-purpose flour
	All-purpose flour	1	(10-ounce) can cream of
2	tablespoons butter		mushroom soup
2	tablespoons vegetable oil	2	cups milk
	Salt and pepper to taste		

Coat the steaks with flour. Brown the steaks in the butter and vegetable oil in a skillet. Season with salt and pepper. Drain on paper towels. Place the steaks in a 9x13-inch baking dish. Add 1/4 cup flour to the drippings in the skillet. Cook until slightly browned, stirring constantly. Add the undiluted soup and milk. Season with additional salt and pepper. Bring to a boil. Cook until slightly thickened, stirring frequently. Pour over the steaks. Bake, covered, at 325 degrees for 1 hour.

Serves 4 to 6

Round steak can be used in this recipe as well. I pound it with a mallet before coating it with flour. You will need to bake round steak longer, but it will be so tender you can cut it with a fork.

CHEESE-STUFFED GIANT BURGER

2 pounds ground round	1/2 teaspoon freshly ground pepper
2 teaspoons dried oregano, crushed	1/4 cup grated Parmesan cheese
1/2 teaspoon dried thyme, crushed	1/4 cup tomato paste
1/2 teaspoon garlic salt	1/4 cup shredded mozzarella cheese

Combine the ground round, oregano, thyme, garlic salt, pepper and Parmesan cheese in a large bowl and mix well. Divide the mixture into halves. Shape each half into an 8-inch patty on waxed paper. Spread the tomato paste over 1 patty, leaving a 1-inch margin. Top with the mozzarella cheese and remaining patty. Press to seal the edges.

Grill over medium coals for 20 minutes. Turn with a wide spatula. Grill for 10 minutes or until cooked through. Do not overcook or it will become dry. Cut into wedges to serve.

Serves 6

GRILLED ROSEMARY PORK

1/3 cup honey mustard	6 (1-inch-thick) pork loin chops,
1/2 cup soy sauce	or 3 to 4 pounds pork
4 to 5 garlic cloves, minced	tenderloin
2 tablespoons minced fresh	
rosemary	

Mix the honey mustard, soy sauce, garlic and rosemary in a small bowl. Combine with the pork chops in a sealable plastic bag. Seal the bag and turn several times to coat the pork. Marinate in the refrigerator for 2 to 4 hours. Remove the pork from the marinade, discarding the remaining marinade.

Grill over medium heat for 14 to 16 minutes or until the pork registers 160 degrees on a meat thermometer, turning the pork once.

Serves 6

SEARED SALMON ON FETTUCCINI

2	(6- to 7-ounce) skinless salmon fillets	1/4	cup chopped onion
	Salt and pepper to taste	4	ounces mushrooms, sliced
1	tablespoon butter	1	tablespoon chopped fresh tarragon
1	quart chicken broth	1/2	cup chicken broth
3	to 4 ounces fettuccini	1/4	cup dry white wine
1	tablespoon butter	4	ounces baby spinach
3	garlic cloves, minced	1/4	cup sour cream

Sprinkle the salmon with salt and pepper. Melt 1 tablespoon butter in a medium skillet over medium-high heat. Sear the salmon in the butter for 2 to 4 minutes per side or until the center is almost opaque. Remove the salmon to a plate and keep warm. Bring 1 quart chicken broth to a boil in a stockpot. Add the fettuccini. Cook just until tender; drain well and keep warm. Melt 1 tablespoon butter in the skillet. Add the garlic, onion, mushrooms and tarragon. Sauté for 3 to 4 minutes. Add 1/2 cup chicken broth and white wine. Cook until the liquid is reduced by 1/2. Add the spinach. Cook for 2 to 3 minutes or until the spinach is wilted, stirring constantly. Remove from the heat. Stir in the sour cream and fettuccini. Arrange fettuccini on warm plates. Top with the salmon. Garnish plates with sprigs of fresh tarragon. Serve immediately.

Serves 2

STUFFING–TOPPED WALLEYE

16	ounces walleye fillets or other mild white fish	2	tablespoons butter, melted
3/4	cup light mayonnaise	2	garlic cloves, minced
3/4	cup shredded sharp Cheddar cheese	1/2	teaspoon sugar
1/3	cup goat cheese	2	tablespoons white wine
		1	cup corn bread stuffing

Arrange the fillets in a single layer in a 9x13-inch baking dish. Bake at 350 degrees for 15 minutes. Mix the mayonnaise, Cheddar cheese, goat cheese, butter, garlic, sugar, wine and stuffing in a bowl. Remove the fish from the oven. Increase the oven temperature to 400 degrees. Spoon the topping mixture evenly over the fish. Bake for 20 minutes or until lightly browned.

Serves 4

Bob's Note: If there is any left, it is very good warmed up the next day. This dish is an instant favorite for anyone we have served it to.

Betty's Note: For a guy who grew up on meat and potatoes, our daughter and I think he has come a long way in his culinary efforts—goat cheese, yet!

BLACK FOREST INN PAN-FRIED CHICKEN

Bernice Musekamp, original owner of the Black Forest Inn, was well known for her delicious fried chicken. While we don't know her recipe, we believe you will enjoy this one. The secrets to great fried chicken are to have the oil hot before you add the chicken so that it doesn't absorb the oil, brown it well, and cook it until it is very tender.

1	(2¹/₂- to 3-pound) chicken, cut up		Salt, pepper and paprika to taste
	All-purpose flour	¹/₄	cup all-purpose flour
¹/₂	cup vegetable oil	2	cups milk

Coat the chicken with flour. Heat ¹/₂ cup vegetable oil to 375 degrees in an electric skillet. Place the chicken pieces carefully in the skillet. Season generously with salt, pepper and paprika. Fry until deep golden brown. Turn and season again. Fry for 30 to 40 minutes or until the crust is deep golden brown and the chicken is cooked through. (If you prefer, you can finish the chicken in the oven once it is browned. Bake, uncovered, at 350 degrees for up to 30 minutes.) Remove to paper towels to drain. For the gravy, drain all but 3 tablespoons vegetable oil from the skillet. Stir in ¹/₄ cup flour. Cook until lightly browned, stirring constantly. Stir in the milk gradually. Cook until bubbly and thickened, stirring constantly. Season with additional salt and pepper.

Serves 4 to 5

SWEET-AND-SOUR CHICKEN AND VEGETABLES

1	(20-ounce) can pineapple chunks	1	tablespoon olive oil
4	carrots	1/4	cup packed brown sugar
1	large onion	1/4	cup ketchup
1	large green bell pepper	2	tablespoons soy sauce
1 1/2	pounds boneless skinless chicken breasts	1	tablespoon rice vinegar
			Hot cooked rice

Drain the pineapple, reserving the juice. Peel the carrots and cut diagonally into 1/4-inch slices. Cut the onion and bell pepper into 1/2-inch pieces. Cut the chicken into 1-inch pieces.

Sauté the chicken in the olive oil in a large ovenproof skillet over high heat. Remove from the heat. Stir in the carrots, onion, bell pepper and pineapple. Mix the reserved pineapple juice, brown sugar, ketchup, soy sauce and vinegar in a bowl. Pour over the chicken and vegetables. Bake, covered, at 350 degrees for 1 hour or until the vegetables are tender. Serve over rice. Freezes well.

Serves 4

GRILLED TURKEY TENDERLOIN

1/4   cup olive oil
1/4   cup soy sauce
1/2   teaspoon basil leaves, crushed
1/2   teaspoon marjoram leaves,
       crushed

1/2   teaspoon thyme leaves, crushed
2   pounds turkey tenderloin or
       turkey cutlets

Mix the olive oil, soy sauce, basil, marjoram and thyme in a large sealable plastic bag. Add the turkey and seal the bag. Turn several times to coat the turkey with the marinade. Marinate in the refrigerator for 2 to 4 hours. Remove the turkey, discarding the remaining marinade. Grill the turkey over medium coals until the turkey registers 165 degrees on a meat thermometer or until the juices run clear.

Serves 5 to 6

TURKEY CRANBERRY PITA POCKETS

This pocket sandwich is also great on hearty wheat bread or with leftover turkey rather than the smoked turkey.

2	ounces cream cheese, softened	2	pita pockets
1/4	cup mayonnaise	4	red lettuce leaves
1	teaspoon sugar	8	large fresh basil leaves
2	tablespoons finely chopped walnuts, toasted	8	slices smoked turkey
1/4	cup whole cranberry sauce		Fresh sprouts

Mix the cream cheese, mayonnaise, sugar, walnuts and cranberry sauce in a bowl. Cut each pita pocket in two. Spread cream cheese mixture inside each pocket. Stuff the pocket with 1 lettuce leaf, 2 basil leaves and 2 turkey slices. Add a generous amount of sprouts to each sandwich. Serve immediately.

Makes 4 sandwiches

PENNE PASTA WITH SUN-DRIED TOMATOES

Serve this easy pasta dish with a green salad and garlic bread for a fantastic fast supper. Make it vegetarian by omitting the sausage or chicken.

1 (14-ounce) can diced tomatoes	8 ounces smoked sausage, sliced, or 2 cooked chicken breasts, cubed
1/3 cup chopped fresh basil	
2 garlic cloves, minced	
1 1/2 tablespoons balsamic vinegar	8 ounces penne pasta, cooked and drained
1/4 cup olive oil	
1/2 teaspoon freshly ground pepper	1/2 cup black olives, sliced
1/2 cup sun-dried tomatoes in oil, chopped	1 1/2 cups mozzarella cheese cubes

For the sauce, mix the diced tomatoes, basil, garlic, vinegar, olive oil, pepper and sun-dried tomatoes in a saucepan. Simmer for 10 minutes. Add the sausage. Simmer until heated through. Combine the pasta and olives in a serving bowl. Pour the sauce over the pasta. Add the cheese and toss lightly.

Serves 4 to 6

ROASTED RED PEPPER AND SHRIMP LINGUINI

1/4 cup (1/2 stick) butter
1   cup sliced mushrooms
3   shallots, thinly sliced
1/4 cup minced fresh basil
1   cup dry white wine
1/4 teaspoon salt
1/8 teaspoon white pepper
1   pound shrimp, peeled,
     deveined, tails removed

4   ounces fresh or frozen
     snow peas
2   red peppers, roasted,
     cut into strips
12   ounces linguini, cooked to
     al dente and drained
1/2 cup freshly grated Parmesan
     cheese
1/4 cup minced fresh parsley

Melt the butter in a large skillet over medium-high heat. Add the mushrooms and shallots. Sauté for 4 to 6 minutes or until tender but not browned. Stir in the basil, wine, salt and pepper. Bring to a boil; reduce the heat. Simmer until the liquid is reduced by 1/2. Add the shrimp. Simmer, covered, for 2 to 3 minutes or until the shrimp turn pink. Stir in the snow peas and peppers. Cook until heated through. Combine with the linguini, cheese and parsley in a bowl and toss gently. Serve with additional Parmesan cheese. You can substitute 2 peppers from a jar of fire-roasted peppers for the fresh peppers if you prefer.

Serves 6 to 8

CAESAR SALAD SANDWICH

This is a modification of a Martha Stewart recipe. It may look like a lot of work, but really it isn't, and the flavors are outstanding.

6	Roma tomatoes, thinly sliced	1/2	cup olive oil
3	tablespoons olive oil	1/4	teaspoon salt
1	tablespoon balsamic vinegar	1/4	teaspoon freshly ground pepper
1/2	teaspoon salt	1/2	teaspoon Dijon mustard
1/8	teaspoon freshly ground pepper	1	head romaine lettuce, rinsed and dried
1	rectangular loaf rustic bread		
1	garlic clove, mashed Juice of 2 lemons	4	ounces Parmigiano-Reggiano cheese, sliced paper-thin

Mix the first 5 ingredients in a bowl. Spread in a single layer on a parchment paper-lined baking sheet. Bake at 250 degrees for 1 hour or until the tomatoes begin to dry. Remove from the oven; let cool. Increase the oven temperature to 375 degrees. Cut the bread lengthwise to but not through the opposite side. Remove most of the crumb so that there is more crust than bread. Bake for 6 minutes or until toasted. Whisk the garlic, lemon juice, 1/2 cup olive oil, 1/4 teaspoon salt, 1/4 teaspoon pepper and Dijon mustard in a bowl. Drizzle a small amount over the opened bread. Toss the remaining dressing with the lettuce and half the cheese. Layer the lettuce, tomato mixture and remaining cheese on the bread. Close the sandwich; slice crosswise into 6 portions.

Serves 6

QUICK TOMATO SAUCE

2 garlic cloves, minced
3 tablespoons olive oil
1/4 teaspoon sugar
1/2 teaspoon salt

1/4 cup chopped fresh basil
1 (28-ounce) can diced tomatoes
1/4 cup drained chopped sun-dried tomatoes

Sauté the garlic in the olive oil in a skillet. Remove from the heat. Stir in the remaining ingredients. Simmer, uncovered, for 20 minutes.

Makes about 3 cups

TERIYAKI MARINADE

1/2 cup soy sauce
1/4 cup water
1/4 cup sugar
2 garlic cloves, minced

1/2 teaspoon ground ginger, or 2 teaspoons minced fresh gingerroot

Mix all ingredients in a bowl, stirring until the sugar is dissolved. Pour over meat or poultry in a sealable plastic bag. Seal the bag and turn several times to coat the meat. Marinate in the refrigerator for 30 minutes to 2 hours. Use for grilled meat or poultry.

Makes about 1 cup

SOUPS AND *side dishes*

CUSTER STATE PARK

CLOSE ENCOUNTERS WITH LOCAL WILDLIFE happen all the time in Custer State Park. It's not unusual to find bison grazing the lawns at the Game Lodge or at the Norbeck Visitor Center. Rocky Mountain bighorn sheep routinely stop cars near park headquarters. The prairie dogs are so bold that close-up photos are easy.

If you get caught in a "buffalo jam," just relax and enjoy the spectacle as hundreds of buffalo cross the highway and block traffic. The bison is the official logo of Custer State Park and is its main claim to fame as a world-class wildlife refuge. Nearly 1,600 buffalo, one of the largest herds anywhere, roam free in the foothills of the 73,000-acre park. The Wildlife Loop Road winds through the prime buffalo range in the southeastern part of the Park, and you'll nearly always find bison here. A buffalo herd is an impressive sight with frolicking calves, matronly cows, and massive bulls that weigh a ton. Despite their mass, the buffalo are agile and quick, and they're absolutely fearless.

Other watchable wildlife includes white-tail deer, pronghorn antelope, mountain goats, and elk. Whether you're a casual sightseer or a serious nature photographer, you will find the critters of Custer State Park put on quite a show. To truly experience the Park, get out and walk some of the hiking trails in the nation's second-largest state park. It includes some of the most spectacular scenery, best wildlife watching, and greatest outdoor recreation that you'll find anywhere.

SOUPS AND SIDE DISHES

CHEESE CHOWDER

1/2	cup shredded carrot	2	cups milk
1/2	cup chopped celery	6	ounces Cheddar cheese,
1/2	cup chopped onion		shredded
2	cups chicken broth		Cheese cubes, such as Cheddar,
3	tablespoons butter, melted		Monterey Jack or Swiss
3	tablespoons all-purpose flour		

Cook the carrot, celery and onion in the chicken broth in a saucepan until tender. Stir in a mixture of the butter and flour. Cook until the broth is slightly thickened, stirring frequently. Add the milk and cook until heated through. Stir in the shredded cheese. Cook until heated through. Place cheese cubes in individual bowls. Ladle the soup into the bowls.

Serves 4

HEARTY POTATO SOUP

This recipe was handed down from my mother. It is chock full of nutritious vegetables, very satisfying on a cold winter night.

3	medium potatoes, peeled and cubed	1/2	cup chopped onion
1	cup chopped broccoli	1	quart chicken broth
1/2	cup chopped cauliflower	2	(12-ounce) cans evaporated milk
1	cup celery, cut into 1/4-inch slices	1	cup cubed cooked ham
2	medium carrots, peeled and chopped or grated	8	ounces Cheddar cheese, shredded
			Salt and pepper to taste

Cook the potatoes, broccoli, cauliflower, celery, carrots and onion in the chicken broth in a stockpot until tender. Stir in the evaporated milk and ham. Cook until heated through. Add the cheese and cook until melted, stirring frequently. Season with salt and pepper.

Serves 10

PUMPKIN SOUP

The sour cream garnish adds a wonderful orange flavor to this soup,
but it is good without it as well.

1/2 medium onion, chopped	1/4 teaspoon pepper
2 tablespoons butter	1 cup half-and-half
2 cups chicken broth	1/4 cup sour cream
1 (15-ounce) can pumpkin (see Note)	1 tablespoon Triple Sec or other orange liqueur (optional)
1/2 teaspoon curry powder	Minced parsley (optional)
1/4 teaspoon salt	

Sauté the onion in the butter in a skillet until tender. Combine with 1/2 cup of the chicken broth in a blender and process until blended and smooth. Combine with the remaining 1 1/2 cups chicken broth, pumpkin, curry powder, salt and pepper in a stockpot and mix well. Cook until heated through; do not boil. Add the half-and-half. Cook until heated through. Mix the sour cream and Triple Sec in a bowl. Ladle the soup into bowls. Top each serving with 2 teaspoons of the sour cream mixture. Sprinkle with parsley.

Note: You can substitute 2 pounds fresh pumpkin if you have it. Cook it in chicken broth and then purée it.

Serves 4

Soups and Side Dishes

CREAMY TOMATO SOUP

3   pounds very ripe tomatoes, peeled
2   carrots, shredded
2   ribs celery, sliced
1   medium onion, chopped
2   tablespoons butter, melted

2   tablespoons all-purpose flour
2   tablespoons sugar
1   teaspoon salt
1/8   teaspoon cayenne pepper, or to taste

Combine the tomatoes, carrots, celery and onion in a medium saucepan and bring to a boil. Simmer until the vegetables are very tender. Process in batches in a blender until smooth. Strain out any remaining tomato seeds if desired and return the mixture to the saucepan. Mix the butter, flour, sugar, salt and cayenne pepper in a small bowl. Sprinkle over the mixture in the saucepan. Cook over low heat until slightly thickened, stirring constantly. Serve hot.

Makes 6 cups

When tomatoes are plentiful in the late summer, I make this soup and cook it down to the consistency of a sauce. It is absolutely wonderful for lasagna or as a base for chili.

HEARTY TOMATO RICE SOUP

1	(28-ounce) can tomatoes	1/4	cup uncooked rice
1	cup chopped onion	1	teaspoon salt
1	cup chopped celery	1	teaspoon chili powder
1	cup chopped carrots	2	bay leaves
2	tablespoons butter	1	cup water

Purée the tomatoes in a blender. Strain through a sieve to remove the seeds. Sauté the onion, celery and carrots in the butter in a large stockpot until tender. Add the tomatoes, rice, salt, chili powder, bay leaves and water. Simmer for 20 to 25 minutes or until the rice is tender. Remove and discard the bay leaves.

For Hearty Beef Tomato Soup, brown 1 pound ground beef with the onions, celery and carrots. Omit the butter, and substitute beef broth for the water. For a chunkier soup, do not purée the tomatoes.

Serves 6

WHITE CHILI

2	tablespoons butter	1	(4-ounce) can chopped green
1/2	cup chopped onion		chiles
2	garlic cloves, minced	2	(15-ounce) cans navy, Great
4	cups chicken broth		Northern or cannellini beans
1	tablespoon chili powder	4	cups chopped cooked chicken
1	tablespoon oregano leaves,		Shredded cheese
	crushed		Sour cream
1	tablespoon cumin		Sliced olives
1/2	teaspoon ground cloves		Sliced avocado
1/2	teaspoon white pepper		Salsa
1/2	teaspoon salt, or to taste		

Melt the butter in a large stockpot over medium heat. Add the onion and garlic. Sauté until the onion is wilted. Remove from the heat. Stir in the chicken broth, chili powder, oregano, cumin, cloves, pepper and salt. Simmer for 15 minutes. Add the green chiles, beans and chicken. Simmer until heated through. Ladle into bowls. Top each serving with cheese, sour cream, olives, avocado or salsa.

Serves 6 to 8

DILLED BEANS AND BROCCOLI

8 ounces green and/or yellow
   beans, trimmed
   Salt to taste
1 cup rice vinegar
1/2 cup vegetable oil
1/4 cup sugar
1 tablespoon dillweed

1/2 teaspoon celery seeds
1/4 teaspoon freshly ground pepper
8 ounces broccoli, cut into
   bite-size pieces
1/2 red bell pepper, cut into
   thin strips
1 medium onion, sliced into rings

Cook the green beans in boiling salted water in a saucepan for 5 minutes or until tender-crisp; drain well. For the dressing, whisk the vinegar, vegetable oil, sugar, dillweed, celery seeds and pepper in a medium bowl until slightly thickened. Combine the green beans, broccoli, bell pepper and onion in a deep salad bowl. Add the dressing and toss to mix. Chill, covered, overnight. Stir again before serving. This is a great picnic dish; it keeps well in the refrigerator for several days.

Serves 6

OLGA'S MAVERICK BEANS

8	ounces small red beans	1/3	cup corn oil or olive oil
2	quarts cold water	1	tablespoon garlic salt
1	small onion, finely chopped		Salt and freshly ground pepper
1/3	cup white vinegar		to taste
1/3	cup dill pickle juice		

Rinse and sort the beans. Combine with the water in a large stockpot. Bring to a boil; reduce the heat. Cook for 1 1/2 hours or until the beans are tender but still firm. Drain well; do not rinse. Combine the beans, onion, vinegar, pickle juice, corn oil and garlic salt in a large bowl and mix well. Season with salt and pepper. May be served warm or marinated in the refrigerator and served cold.

Makes 1 quart

These beans were served in small bowls on the table as a before-dinner relish at the Maverick Supper Club in Sheridan, Wyoming. Although all the food was outstanding, the beans were one of the main reasons for going. Sadly, the Maverick has burned.

PICNIC BEANS

8	ounces bacon	4	ounces sharp Cheddar cheese, cubed
1	medium onion, chopped		
1/2	cup packed brown sugar	1	can lima beans, drained
1/2	cup ketchup	1	can garbanzo beans, drained
1	teaspoon vinegar	1	can kidney beans, drained
1	tablespoon Worcestershire sauce		

Cook the bacon in a skillet until crisp; drain well, reserving 1 tablespoon drippings. Crumble the bacon and set aside. Sauté the onion in the drippings in the skillet until tender. Add the brown sugar, ketchup, vinegar and Worcestershire sauce and mix well. Combine the onion mixture, bacon, cheese, lima beans, garbanzo beans and kidney beans in a large bowl and mix well. Spoon into a large casserole sprayed with nonstick cooking spray. Bake at 350 degrees for 1 hour or until bubbly and heated through. May instead be heated on Low in a slow cooker for 3 to 4 hours.

Serves 10 to 12

RED POTATOES WITH GORGONZOLA CHEESE

2	pounds red potatoes, cut into halves		1/4	cup sour cream
1/2	teaspoon salt		4	ounces Gorgonzola cheese, crumbled
1/4	cup buttermilk		1	tablespoon minced fresh chives
1/4	cup (1/2 stick) butter or margarine			Salt and freshly ground pepper to taste

Combine the potatoes and 1/2 teaspoon salt with water to cover in a medium saucepan. Bring to a boil; reduce the heat. Simmer, covered, for 15 to 20 minutes or until tender; drain well. Combine the buttermilk, butter, sour cream and cheese in a microwave-safe bowl. Microwave for 1 to 2 minutes or just until the chill is off. Lightly mash the potatoes in the saucepan. Stir in the buttermilk mixture. Spoon into a serving dish. Sprinkle with the chives, salt and pepper.

Serves 6

BERYL'S SCALLOPED POTATOES

9   *medium potatoes, sliced*
1   *medium carrot, grated*
1/2 *medium onion, sliced, or*
    1/4 cup dried onion

Salt and pepper to taste
3   *cups heavy cream*

Arrange the potatoes, carrot and onion in a 9x12-inch baking pan sprayed with nonstick cooking spray. Season with salt and pepper. Pour the cream over the top. Bake at 350 degrees for 1 hour. Remove from the oven and press the potatoes down into the cream. Bake for 30 minutes or until the potatoes are tender and the top is lightly browned.

Serves 6 to 8

SPINACH ARTICHOKE CASSEROLE

2	packages frozen chopped spinach, thawed and drained	1	(10-ounce) can cream of celery soup
1	(6-ounce) jar marinated artichoke hearts	4	eggs, beaten
2	tablespoons butter	1/8	teaspoon freshly ground pepper
1	medium onion, chopped	1	(2-ounce) jar pimento
1/4	teaspoon ground nutmeg	8	ounces cream cheese, softened
1	teaspoon oregano leaves	1/3	cup milk
		1/3	cup grated Parmesan cheese

Squeeze the moisture from the spinach. Drain the artichoke hearts, reserving
2 tablespoons of the marinade. Chop the artichoke hearts. Heat the reserved marinade
with the butter in a large skillet over medium heat. Add the onion. Cook until the onion
is wilted, stirring constantly. Stir in the spinach, artichoke hearts, nutmeg, oregano,
undiluted soup, eggs, pepper and pimento. Spoon into a greased shallow 2-quart
baking dish. Beat the cream cheese, milk and Parmesan cheese in a bowl. Spread over
the spinach mixture. Bake at 325 degrees for 35 minutes or until the center feels firm
when lightly pressed.

Serves 8

SUMMER SQUASH

2   pounds yellow and/or green
    summer squash, cut into
    ⅛-inch slices
½   cup chopped onion
    Salt to taste
1   cup sour cream

1   (10-ounce) can cream of
    chicken soup
1   cup shredded carrot
1   (8-ounce) package
    herb-seasoned stuffing mix
¼   cup (½ stick) butter, melted

Cook the squash and onion in boiling salted water in a saucepan for 5 minutes; drain. Combine the sour cream, undiluted soup and carrot in a large bowl. Stir in the squash mixture. Mix the stuffing mix and butter in a small bowl. Spread half the stuffing in a 2-quart baking dish sprayed with nonstick cooking spray. Top with the vegetable mixture. Sprinkle remaining stuffing over the vegetables. Bake at 350 degrees for 25 to 35 minutes or until heated through.

Serves 6

I would like to give credit to the magazine that printed this recipe years ago, but my copy is so worn that I can't read it any longer. When zucchini and yellow squash are plentiful, I make several casseroles and freeze them to enjoy in the winter. Other vegetables can be added or substituted for some of the squash.

LEMON DILL VEGGIES

A very colorful side dish

8	ounces carrots, peeled
8	ounces zucchini
8	ounces yellow squash
1	red bell pepper, cored and seeded
2	tablespoons butter

1/4	cup chicken broth
	Juice of 1/2 lemon
1	tablespoon chopped fresh dill, or 1 teaspoon dried dillweed
	Salt and freshly ground pepper to taste

Julienne the carrots, zucchini and squash or cut diagonally into 1/8-inch slices. Cut the bell pepper into strips. Melt the butter in a large skillet over medium heat. Add the carrots, zucchini, squash and bell pepper, stirring until coated. Sauté for 4 to 5 minutes or until tender-crisp. Stir in the chicken broth, lemon juice and dill. Cook to the desired degree of doneness. Season with salt and pepper.

Serves 6

FRESH VEGGIE SAUTÉ

2	tablespoons olive oil	1/4	cup coarsely chopped fresh basil
1	medium onion, thinly sliced		Salt and pepper to taste
4	cups sliced zucchini	1/4	cup grated Parmesan cheese
8	ounces mushrooms, sliced		(optional)
4	or 5 Roma tomatoes, quartered		

Heat the olive oil in a large skillet over medium-high heat. Add the onion. Cook for 3 to 4 minutes, stirring frequently. Add the zucchini. Cook until the zucchini begins to wilt. Add the mushrooms. Cook until almost tender. Stir in the tomatoes, basil, salt and pepper. Cook to desired degree of doneness. Spoon into a serving dish. Sprinkle with the cheese.

Serves 4

CORN SPOON BREAD

2	eggs		1	can whole kernel corn
1	cup sour cream		1	can cream-style corn
1	(7-ounce) package corn muffin mix		1/3	cup butter, melted

Beat the eggs lightly in a bowl. Stir in the sour cream, muffin mix, undrained whole kernel corn and cream-style corn. Add the butter and mix well. Spoon into a 1 1/2-quart baking dish sprayed with nonstick cooking spray. Bake at 350 degrees for 30 to 40 minutes or until a knife inserted near the center comes out clean.

Serves 8 to 10

A great cook gave this recipe to me years ago at a church supper. It has become a tradition at holiday meals at our house and a requested favorite whenever family gathers. If prepared ahead and refrigerated until baking time, bake for an additional 10 to 15 minutes. A flat baking dish works best.

POLENTA

*This is a very easy way to prepare polenta, eliminating standing at the
stove and stirring constantly.*

1	cup polenta	1/4	cup (1/2 stick) butter
3	cups chicken broth	1/2	cup grated Parmesan cheese
	Salt and pepper to taste		

Whisk the polenta and chicken broth in a 2-quart microwave-safe bowl. Microwave,
covered with plastic wrap, on High for 12 minutes. Season with salt and pepper and
stir several times. Stir in the butter and cheese. Spoon into a buttered 2-quart
casserole. Bake at 350 degrees until heated through. Serve with pot roast,
beef stew or lamb.

Serves 4

*The polenta and chicken broth mixture can be used in other
recipes calling for polenta.*

WILD RICE STUFFING

1	can chicken broth	1/2	teaspoon dried rosemary, crushed
1/4	cup uncooked wild rice	1/2	teaspoon dried sage leaves, crushed
1	cup chopped celery		
1	cup chopped onion	1/4	teaspoon salt
1/2	cup shredded carrots	1/4	teaspoon pepper
2	tablespoons chopped parsley	4	cups dry bread cubes
2	tablespoons butter, melted		
1/2	teaspoon dried basil		

Combine the chicken broth and wild rice in a slow cooker. Cook on High for 3 hours. Add the celery, onion, carrots, parsley, butter, basil, rosemary, sage, salt, pepper and bread cubes. Cook on Low for 4 hours.

To prepare in the oven, simmer the wild rice in the chicken broth until almost tender. Mix with the remaining ingredients and spoon into a greased baking pan. Bake at 350 degrees for 1 hour.

Serves 6

Any bread will work in this recipe; I like a hearty one, such as French or Italian. I often add some whole wheat bread as well.

COOKIES AND *desserts*

DEVIL'S TOWER

THE TIMBERED MOUNTAINS OF THE Black Hills National Forest continue ten to forty miles beyond the South Dakota border, westward into Wyoming. In the north, there is a distinct branch of the Black Hills known as the Bear Lodge district. This is the home of Devil's Tower National Monument. The two-square-mile park surrounding the tower was proclaimed the nation's first national monument by President Theodore Roosevelt in 1906. The Tower is a solitary, stump-shaped granite formation that looms 865 feet above the tree-lined Belle Fourche River Valley, like a skyscraper in the country. It's the core of an ancient volcano. The mountain's markings are the basis for a Native American legend. This Kiowa legend tells of seven sisters and a brother. When the brother was magically transformed into a giant bear, the sisters ran for their lives. They climbed a nearby tree stump, which began to rise to the sky. The bear clawed at the bark of the tree, trying to reach the seven maidens, but failed. The sisters ascended into the sky and became the stars of the Big Dipper. The bear's claw marks still show on the Tower. The stone pillar is about 1,000 feet in diameter at the bottom and 275 feet at the top, and that makes it the premier rock-climbing challenge in the Black Hills. Approximately 5,000 climbers come here every year from all over the world to climb on the massive columns.

COOKIES AND DESSERTS

CASHEW COOKIES

This is a soft, rich, cake-like cookie that I think you will agree is worth the extra effort of frosting them with Brown Butter Frosting. They are great with coffee.

2¹/2 cups all-purpose flour	2 teaspoons vanilla extract
1 teaspoon baking soda	1 cup sour cream
¹/2 teaspoon baking powder	1 cup chopped cashews
¹/2 teaspoon salt	¹/4 cup (¹/2 stick) butter
¹/2 cup (1 stick) butter, softened	2 tablespoons hot water
1¹/4 cups packed brown sugar	1 teaspoon vanilla
2 eggs	2 cups confectioners' sugar, sifted

Mix the flour, baking soda, baking powder and salt together. Cream ¹/2 cup butter and brown sugar in a mixer bowl until light and fluffy. Add the eggs, 2 teaspoons vanilla and sour cream and mix well. Add the flour mixture gradually, beating well after each addition. Stir in the cashews. Drop by teaspoonfuls onto parchment paper-lined or greased cookie sheets. Bake at 375 degrees for 8 to 10 minutes. Let stand until cool. For Brown Butter Frosting, heat ¹/4 cup butter in a saucepan until golden brown. Remove from the heat. Add the hot water, 1 teaspoon vanilla and confectioners' sugar and mix well.

Makes 4¹/2 dozen

CHOCOLATE CRINKLES

2³/4 cups all-purpose flour
2 teaspoons baking powder
¹/2 teaspoon salt
¹/2 cup vegetable oil
4 ounces unsweetened chocolate, melted

2 cups sugar
4 eggs
2 teaspoons vanilla extract
1 teaspoon almond extract
Confectioners' sugar or sugar

Mix the flour, baking powder and salt together. Mix the vegetable oil and chocolate in a bowl. Add the sugar. Blend in the eggs and flavorings. Add the flour mixture and mix well. Shape into 1-inch balls and roll in confectioners' sugar. Place on parchment paper-lined cookie sheets or cookie sheets sprayed with nonstick cooking spray. Bake at 350 degrees for 10 to 12 minutes or until golden brown; do not overbake.

Makes 5 to 6 dozen cookies

CHOCOLATE CHIP COOKIES

This recipe is a modified version of one printed in Cook's Illustrated. *It makes a large batch, but they freeze well baked or unbaked. The secret to the success of this thick, chewy, delicious cookie is the melted butter.*

6¹/₂ cups bleached flour
1¹/₂ teaspoons salt
1¹/₂ teaspoons baking soda
2 cups (4 sticks) unsalted butter, melted
3 cups packed brown sugar

1¹/₂ cups sugar
3 large eggs
3 egg yolks
2 tablespoons vanilla extract
4 cups chocolate chips

Mix the flour, salt and baking soda together. Mix the butter, brown sugar and sugar in a large bowl. Add the eggs, egg yolks and vanilla and mix well. Add the flour mixture gradually, stirring just until mixed. Stir in the chocolate chips. Shape into irregularly shaped mounds (not smooth balls). Place 2 inches apart on parchment paper-lined cookie sheets. Bake at 325 degrees for 14 to 16 minutes or until golden brown. Rotate the cookie sheet from the bottom to the top rack about halfway through the baking time. Cool slightly on the cookie sheets. Remove to a wire rack to cool completely. Store in an airtight container.

Makes 6 dozen large cookies

MINT CHOCOLATE MINIATURE SANDWICH COOKIES

These delightful little cookies are a real treat with a glass of cold milk or with ice cream or sherbet.

2   cups all-purpose flour
2   teaspoons baking soda
1/4 teaspoon salt
2/3 cup margarine, softened
1/2 cup sugar
1   large egg

1   cup semisweet chocolate chips, melted
1/4 cup light corn syrup
     Sugar
     Thin mints

Mix the flour, baking soda and salt together. Beat the margarine and sugar in a mixer bowl until light and fluffy. Beat in the egg. Add the chocolate and corn syrup and mix well. Add the flour mixture 1/4 at a time, beating well after each addition. Chill, covered, for 3 hours to overnight. Shape the dough by teaspoonfuls into balls. Roll in additional sugar. Place 2 inches apart on an ungreased cookie sheet. Place no more than 20 on a cookie sheet; the cookies will cool quickly and must be quite hot to melt the mints. Bake at 350 degrees for 12 to 14 minutes; do not overbake. Place the cookie sheet on a wire rack. When the cookies are cool enough to handle, sandwich 1 thin mint between 2 baked cookies. Let stand until cool. These cookies freeze well. They can be eaten straight from the freezer or allowed to thaw.

Makes 5 dozen "sandwiches"

BROWNIES

I have used this recipe for at least 20 years, and it cannot be beaten for taste or ease of preparation.

1	cup (2 sticks) butter or margarine		$^{1}/_{4}$	cup ($^{1}/_{2}$ stick) butter, softened
$^{1}/_{2}$	cup baking cocoa		$^{1}/_{4}$	cup baking cocoa
2	cups sugar		2	to 3 tablespoons milk or half-and-half
4	eggs		1	teaspoon vanilla extract
$1^{1}/_{2}$	cups all-purpose flour		$^{1}/_{4}$	teaspoon salt
1	teaspoon salt		$1^{1}/_{4}$	to $1^{1}/_{2}$ cups confectioners' sugar
1	teaspoon vanilla extract			

Melt 1 cup butter in a saucepan. Add $^{1}/_{2}$ cup baking cocoa; mix well. Remove from the heat. Stir in the sugar and eggs. Add the flour, 1 teaspoon salt and 1 teaspoon vanilla; mix well. Spoon into a greased 9x13-inch baking pan. Bake at 350 degrees for 20 to 25 minutes. Let stand until cool. For Chocolate Frosting, combine $^{1}/_{4}$ cup butter, $^{1}/_{4}$ cup baking cocoa, milk, 1 teaspoon vanilla, $^{1}/_{4}$ teaspoon salt and confectioners' sugar in a bowl and mix until of spreading consistency. Spread over the cookies.

Makes 16

MELTAWAYS

Trust the time given on these cookies; they do not brown. The frosting needs to be soft, as the cookies are easily broken. Not the cookies to send in the mail, but the perfect cookie for a shower, tea, or special treat.

2   cups (4 sticks) butter, softened
1¹/2 cups cornstarch
²/3 cup confectioners' sugar
2   cups all-purpose flour
2   tablespoons butter, softened
3   tablespoons milk

1   teaspoon almond or vanilla extract
2¹/2 cups sifted confectioners' sugar
¹/8 teaspoon salt
    Food coloring (optional)

Mix 2 cups butter, cornstarch, confectioners' sugar and 2 cups flour in a bowl. Shape into 1-inch balls. Place on parchment paper-lined or ungreased cookie sheets. Bake at 325 degrees for 15 minutes. Let stand until cool. Combine 2 tablespoons butter, milk, almond extract, confectioners' sugar and salt in a bowl and mix well. Stir in the food coloring. Spread over the cookies.

Makes 5 dozen

NO-BAKE PEANUT BARS

This was one of my mother's recipes. It's very quick, and the kids love it.

1	cup confectioners' sugar	2	cups butterscotch chips
1	cup chopped peanuts	1	cup evaporated milk
2	cups miniature marshmallows	1/2	cup peanut butter
4	cups graham cracker crumbs	1/3	cup finely chopped peanuts

Mix the confectioners' sugar, 1 cup peanuts, marshmallows and graham cracker crumbs in a large bowl. Combine the butterscotch chips and evaporated milk in a saucepan. Heat until the butterscotch chips are melted. Add the peanut butter and blend well. Pour over the marshmallow mixture; stir just until moistened. Spoon into a buttered 9x13-inch baking pan. Sprinkle 1/3 cup peanuts over the top. Chill thoroughly and cut into bars.

Makes 24 bars

SALTED PEANUT COOKIES

*These cookies spread thin as they bake, becoming almost lacy.
They have a wonderful butterscotch flavor.*

1³/₄ cups all-purpose flour	1 cup (2 sticks) butter, softened
1 teaspoon baking soda	3 eggs
1 teaspoon baking powder	3¹/₂ cups rolled oats
1 cup sugar	1¹/₂ cups dry-roasted peanuts
1 cup packed brown sugar	

Mix the flour, baking soda and baking powder together. Cream the sugar, brown sugar and butter in a mixer bowl until light and fluffy. Add the eggs and mix well. Add the flour mixture gradually, beating well after each addition. Stir in the oats and peanuts.

Drop the batter by tablespoonfuls onto greased or parchment paper-lined cookie sheets (about 8 cookies to each cookie sheet).

Bake at 375 degrees for 8 to 10 minutes or until the edges are golden brown and the center is set. Do not overbake. Let stand to cool slightly. Remove to a wire rack to cool completely.

Makes about 4 dozen large cookies

SNICKERDOODLES

2   tablespoons sugar
2   teaspoons cinnamon
2$^{1}/_{4}$ cups all-purpose flour
2   teaspoons cream of tartar
1$^{1}/_{4}$ teaspoons baking soda

$^{1}/_{2}$ teaspoon salt
1   cup shortening
1$^{1}/_{2}$ cups sugar
2   eggs

Mix 2 tablespoons sugar and cinnamon in a shallow dish. Mix the flour, cream of tartar, baking soda and salt together. Cream the shortening and 1$^{1}/_{2}$ cups sugar in a mixer bowl until light and fluffy. Beat in the eggs. Add the flour mixture $^{1}/_{2}$ at a time, beating well after each addition. Shape into walnut-size balls. Roll in the cinnamon mixture. Place on ungreased or parchment paper-lined cookie sheets. Bake at 400 degrees for 8 to 10 minutes. At altitudes above 5,000 feet, use $^{1}/_{4}$ cup more flour.

Makes 3 dozen cookies

TOFFEE ALMOND SANDIES

3¹/4 cups all-purpose flour
1   teaspoon baking soda
1   teaspoon cream of tartar
1   teaspoon salt
1   cup (2 sticks) butter, softened
1   cup sugar
1   cup packed brown sugar

¹/2 cup vegetable oil
2   eggs
1   teaspoon almond extract
1   cup chopped almonds
6   ounces English toffee bits
     Grated zest of 1 orange
     Sugar

Mix the flour, baking soda, cream of tartar and salt together. Cream the butter, 1 cup sugar and brown sugar in a mixer bowl until light and fluffy. Add the vegetable oil, eggs and almond extract and mix well. Add the flour mixture gradually, mixing well after each addition. Stir in the almonds, toffee bits and orange zest. Shape into 1-inch balls. Roll in additional sugar. Place on ungreased cookie sheets. Flatten with a fork. Bake at 350 degrees for 12 to 14 minutes or until lightly browned.

Makes 12 dozen cookies

UNBELIEVABLE COOKIES

1   cup sugar
1   cup chunky peanut butter
1   egg

1/2   cup rolled oats
      Sugar

Blend 1 cup sugar into the peanut butter in a bowl. Add the egg and oats and mix well. Shape into small balls and dip in additional sugar. Place on greased or parchment paper-lined cookie sheets. Flatten with a fork. Bake at 350 degrees for 10 minutes. Cool on a wire rack.

Makes 1¹/₂ dozen cookies

These cookies are so quick and easy to make that, 20 minutes after you start them, they will be hot and fresh from the oven when the kids come home from school or the guests arrive at the door. Because they are so easy to make, I am always amazed at the number of people who ask for the recipe.

ENGLISH APPLE PIE

1/2	cup all-purpose flour	3/4	cup sugar
1	teaspoon baking powder	1	teaspoon vanilla extract
1	teaspoon cinnamon	1/2	cup chopped walnuts
1/4	teaspoon salt	1	cup chopped unpeeled baking
1	egg		apples

Mix the flour, baking powder, cinnamon and salt together. Beat the egg in a large bowl. Add the sugar and beat until light and foamy. Add the flour mixture and mix well. Stir in the vanilla, walnuts and apples.

Spoon into a greased 9-inch pie plate. Bake at 350 degrees for 25 to 30 minutes or until a knife inserted near the center comes out clean. Serve with ice cream.

Serves 6

Try baking this unique no-crust pie in the fall when fresh apples are plentiful.
Preparation time is only about 10 minutes, and the taste is superb.

BUTTERSCOTCH PIE

*Several people have told us how good Bernice Musekamp's
butterscotch pie was. This is a close replica of her recipe.*

4	egg yolks	2	cups milk
1/2	cup evaporated milk	1	teaspoon vanilla extract
1/4	cup cornstarch	1	baked (9-inch) pie shell, cooled
1/4	teaspoon salt	1	cup whipping cream
1/3	cup butter	1	teaspoon vanilla extract
1	cup packed brown sugar	1	to 2 tablespoons sugar, or to taste

Beat the egg yolks in a bowl. Stir in the evaporated milk, cornstarch and salt. Heat the butter in a medium saucepan over medium heat until melted and golden brown; do not burn. Reduce the heat to medium-low. Add the brown sugar. Cook for 5 minutes or until dark golden brown, stirring constantly. Add the milk. Cook until the brown sugar dissolves, stirring constantly. Whisk in the cornstarch mixture gradually. Increase the heat to medium. Boil for 1 minute. Remove from heat. Stir in 1 teaspoon vanilla. Place waxed paper directly on top of the filling. Let stand for 30 minutes or until cooled. Pour into the pie shell. Chill, covered with plastic wrap, in the refrigerator for 3 hours. Beat the whipping cream in a mixer bowl until soft peaks form. Beat in 1 teaspoon vanilla. Add the sugar gradually, beating until dissolved. Spread the whipped cream over the pie filling.

Serves 6 to 8

MOCHA FUDGE ICE CREAM PIE

18	Oreo cookies, crushed	1/2	teaspoon almond extract
1/4	cup (1/2 stick) butter, melted	1	quart coffee ice cream, softened
3	ounces semisweet chocolate, melted	1	cup whipping cream
1/4	cup (1/2 stick) butter	2	tablespoons confectioners' sugar
2/3	cup sugar	1	teaspoon vanilla extract
2/3	cup evaporated milk	1/2	cup chopped pecans

Mix the cookie crumbs and melted butter in a bowl. Press into a 10-inch pie plate. Chill until needed. For the sauce, mix the chocolate, 1/4 cup butter, sugar and evaporated milk in a saucepan. Bring to a boil. Simmer for 4 to 5 minutes. Remove from the heat. Stir in the almond extract. Let cool to room temperature.

Spoon the ice cream into the chilled crust. Top with the sauce. Freeze until needed. Beat the whipping cream in a mixer bowl until soft peaks form. Add the confectioners' sugar and vanilla and beat until stiff peaks form. Spread over the pie. Sprinkle with the pecans. Freeze until firm. Let stand for 20 minutes before serving. Can be wrapped in foil and frozen for up to 4 weeks. To substitute vanilla ice cream for the coffee ice cream, dissolve 1 tablespoon instant coffee granules in 1 tablespoon hot water. Stir into the softened vanilla ice cream.

Serves 6

PECAN PIE

3	eggs	1/3	cup butter, melted and slightly cooled
1	cup light corn syrup		
1	cup packed dark brown sugar	1	unbaked (9-inch) pie shell
1/4	teaspoon salt	1	cup pecan halves
2	teaspoons vanilla extract		

Beat the eggs in a large bowl. Add the corn syrup, brown sugar, salt, vanilla and butter and mix well. Spoon into the pie shell. Arrange the pecans spoke-fashion over the top. Bake at 350 degrees for 45 minutes or until a knife inserted near the center comes out clean.

Serves 6

For recipes that call for toasted pecans, place the pecans on a baking sheet, and bake at 375 degrees for 5 to 8 minutes, stirring several times. They will burn if neglected, so set the timer!

GRAMMA'S PEACH PIE

1	(2-crust) pie pastry	1/2	teaspoon freshly ground nutmeg
4	cups peeled and sliced fresh peaches	1/4	teaspoon salt
		2	tablespoons butter
1	cup sugar	2	teaspoons milk
3	tablespoons all-purpose flour	1	tablespoon sugar

Fit 1 pastry into a pie plate. Combine the peaches, 1 cup sugar, flour, nutmeg and salt in a bowl and toss to coat the peaches. Spoon into the pie plate. Dot with the butter. Cover with the remaining pastry, fluting to seal the edge. Cut 2 to 3 slits in the top for vents. Brush the top with milk; sprinkle with 1 tablespoon sugar. Bake at 400 degrees for 40 to 45 minutes or until golden brown. May omit the butter and the top crust and use this Crumb Topping: Mix 1/2 cup sugar, 1/3 cup butter and 3/4 cup all-purpose flour and sprinkle over the pie before baking.

Serves 6

My husband's grandmother was a master with a little pie dough and fruit of any kind. One of my favorite memories of her is stopping by her house one evening about 7:30 to find her in her little kitchen "stirring up a pie" just because that's what she was hungry for!

PUMPKIN ICE CREAM PIE

1	pint vanilla ice cream, softened	1/2	teaspoon ginger
1	baked (9-inch) crumb crust	1/2	teaspoon cinnamon
1	cup canned pumpkin	1/2	teaspoon salt
3/4	cup sugar	1	cup whipping cream, whipped
1/2	teaspoon nutmeg	1/2	cup chopped pecans

Spoon the ice cream into the cooled crust. Mix the pumpkin, sugar, nutmeg, ginger, cinnamon, salt and whipped cream in a bowl. Spread over the ice cream. Sprinkle with the pecans. Freeze until firm. Let stand for several minutes before serving. May be frozen for up to 1 month. May substitute 2 cups whipped topping for the whipped cream; reduce the sugar to 1/2 cup.

Serves 8

RHUBARB CUSTARD PIE

2	cups sugar	4	cups rhubarb, cut into
1/4	cup all-purpose flour		1/2-inch pieces
3/4	teaspoon nutmeg	1	unbaked (9-inch) pie shell
3	eggs, lightly beaten		Crumb Topping (page 129)
3	tablespoons milk		

Mix the sugar, flour and nutmeg together. Combine the eggs and milk in a large bowl. Add the flour mixture and mix well. Arrange the rhubarb in the pie shell. Spoon the egg mixture over the fruit. Top with Crumb Topping. Bake at 400 degrees for 50 to 60 minutes or until a knife inserted near the center comes out clean.

Serves 6

RASPBERRY RHUBARB CRISP

1/2 cup packed brown sugar	1 teaspoon minced fresh
2 1/2 tablespoons cornstarch	rosemary
1/2 teaspoon nutmeg	1/2 cup all-purpose flour
3 cups rhubarb, cut into	1/2 cup rolled oats
1/2-inch slices	1/2 cup packed brown sugar
1 cup fresh or individually frozen	1/8 teaspoon salt
raspberries	1/4 cup (1/2 stick) butter, melted

Mix 1/2 cup brown sugar, cornstarch and nutmeg in a large bowl. Stir in the rhubarb, raspberries and rosemary. Spoon into a 2-quart baking dish sprayed with nonstick cooking spray. Mix the flour, oats, 1/2 cup brown sugar and salt in a medium bowl. Stir in the butter. Crumble over the fruit mixture. Bake at 375 degrees for 25 to 30 minutes or until the rhubarb is tender. If the fruit is tender but the top has not browned, bake at 400 degrees for 5 minutes. Serve warm with ice cream or whipped cream.

Serves 6 to 8

CHOCOLATE RASPBERRY TRIFLE

8	ounces Milky Way bars, chopped	1/3	to 1/2 cup raspberry preserves
1/3	cup milk	1/2	cup orange juice
1	(10- to 11-ounce) frozen pound cake, thawed	11/4	cups whipping cream, whipped Fresh raspberries

Combine the candy and milk in a microwave-safe bowl. Microwave until the candy is melted. Let cool to room temperature. Cut the cake into 24 equal slices. Spread half the cake slices with preserves; top with the remaining slices. Wrap and reserve 2 cake "sandwiches;" chill until needed.

Cover the bottom of a 6-cup trifle dish or other glass bowl with half the remaining cake sandwiches. Drizzle with half the orange juice. Fold the cooled candy mixture into about 2 cups of the whipped cream, swirling to create a marbled effect. Spoon half the candy mixture over the cake slices in the trifle dish. Repeat the layers. Chill, covered, for 6 hours to overnight. Cut each reserved cake sandwich lengthwise into 3 strips. Arrange over the top in a pinwheel design. Garnish with the remaining 1/2 cup whipped cream and raspberries.

Serves 8 to 10

LEMON CHEESECAKE

This light and luscious dessert has been a favorite of our family for many years. It can be prepared a day ahead.

10	tablespoons butter, melted	1	cup boiling water
2¹/₂	cups graham cracker crumbs	1	cup sugar
2	tablespoons confectioners' sugar	8	ounces cream cheese, softened
		2	teaspoons vanilla extract
1	small package lemon gelatin	1	cup very cold evaporated milk

Mix the butter, graham cracker crumbs and confectioners' sugar in a bowl. Reserve 1 cup of the mixture. Pat the remaining crumb mixture into a 9x13-inch pan. Dissolve the gelatin in the boiling water in a bowl. Add the sugar, stirring until dissolved. Chill until needed. Beat the cream cheese and vanilla in a mixer bowl until light and fluffy. Add the gelatin mixture gradually, mixing well after each addition. Beat the evaporated milk in a large mixer bowl until very stiff. Fold in the gelatin mixture. Spoon over the crumb crust in the pan. Top with the reserved crumbs. Chill for 3 hours or longer.

Serves 12

MILLION-DOLLAR FUDGE

This great-tasting fudge is exceptionally smooth and very quick to make.
Our family requests it every time we get together.

12	ounces semisweet chocolate chips	2	cups chopped pecans (optional)
1	pint marshmallow creme	4^1/$_2$	cups sugar
2	(7-ounce) Hershey bars, chopped	^{1}/$_4$	cup (^{1}/$_2$ stick) butter
		1	(12-ounce) can evaporated milk
		^{1}/$_4$	teaspoon salt

Mix the chocolate chips, marshmallow creme, candy and pecans in a large bowl. Combine the sugar, butter, evaporated milk and salt in a buttered heavy saucepan. Bring to a boil over medium heat, stirring frequently. Boil for 4^1/$_2$ minutes. Pour over the chocolate mixture, stirring until the chocolate is melted. Pour into a buttered 9x13-inch dish.

Makes about 4 pounds

GRAMMA'S FAMOUS CHOCOLATE SAUCE

This sauce, served over unfrosted white cake, was a favorite standby dessert at my mother-in-law's bountiful table. She sometimes made a cake from scratch, but often used a cake mix so that this could be a "quick fix" for unexpected company or for her hungry family and the hired ranch hands.

4	cups sugar	$^1/_8$	teaspoon salt
$^1/_2$	cup baking cocoa	3	tablespoons butter
$^1/_2$	cup light corn syrup	2	teaspoons vanilla extract
1	(12-ounce) can evaporated milk		

Butter the bottom and side of a medium heavy saucepan. Combine the sugar, baking cocoa, corn syrup, evaporated milk and salt in the saucepan. Bring to a boil over medium-high heat, stirring constantly. Reduce the heat to medium. Simmer for 2 minutes, stirring only if necessary to prevent sticking. Remove from the heat. Stir in the butter and vanilla. Serve warm. This is very good over unfrosted white cake slices that have been topped with vanilla ice cream.

Serves 15

CONTRIBUTORS

Rebecca Barkley

Steve Barkley

Sue Birkholz

Beryl Bushong

Sally Cook

Bev Cochran

Lauriena Curtis

Corky Foley

Jan Harrison

Karen Lidahl

Eunice McEwan

Wendy Mort

Alma Reder

Florence Reder

Geoffrey Ritchie

Nancy Roth

Nancy Taylor

Sandy Walters

Carolyn Walton

HELPFUL HINTS

I make my shopping lists on a large envelope. On one side, I list the places I need to go; my grocery list goes on the other side. Receipts, bank deposits, etc., go inside the envelope.

I keep a Post-it Note pad where I do my food and baking prep to jot down things I am low on, so that they actually make it to my grocery list.

If you use many different cookbooks or cooking magazines and can't remember where you found a particular recipe, you might try one of these methods. List the recipe on a recipe card, where you found it, when you served it and to whom, and file it in your recipe file. If you don't want to take the time to do that, you can mark the page with a Post-it flag or a paper clip. I also highlight favorite recipes in the index with a yellow highlighter. Any of these methods will help find those elusive recipes you have tried once but can't find again. I am currently searching for one I still can't find. (Do as I say, not as I do.)

I buy most of my spices in bulk, but in small amounts. They are much more economical and fresher. For storing spices, I have a spice rack that displays the spices lying in a drawer, which I love because I can read the labels easily. I alphabetize them so they are easy to find. (Sometimes little people who are visiting rearrange them, but this Nana thinks that is OK. One of the joys of being a gramma, don't you think?)

If you don't have a drawer you can devote to spices, those stacking turntables or graduated-height storage racks work pretty well, if you organize in some manner—alphabetically, savory herbs/spices for baking, etc. If you keep spices in a drawer so that you see just the tops, you might try labeling the lids with stickers giving their names and the date you bought them. However you store spices, they retain their quality only for about a year—another reason to buy them in small quantities.

I use parchment paper for lining baking sheets for cookies, scones, biscuits, etc. I love to cook. I don't love to wash dishes. Using parchment paper produces nice results and saves on dishwashing. The paper can now be bought in supermarkets and kitchen stores in rolls like waxed paper. If you can't find it there, some supermarket bakeries will sell it by the sheet.

Turbinado sugar is a coarse natural sugar that makes a great topping for muffins.

I use a strainer for sifting confectioners' sugar. It is easy to use and to wash.

Try putting a vanilla bean in a jar of sugar to use for sweetening fruit or drinks. Just split the bean, put it in a jar, and add sugar.

I buy unsalted butter on sale and freeze it. Using unsalted butter is one of the best ways to control the amount of salt in a recipe.

I place coarse salt in a small bowl and use it to season food while I am cooking. I think the coarse salt tastes better, and I can better control the amount when I use my fingers for adding a pinch of salt.

Find a good-quality olive oil. It makes all the difference in salads and sautéed foods.

Some things are just better fresh, for example, freshly ground black pepper, freshly grated Parmesan cheese, and freshly grated nutmeg. If you can, use fresh herbs. Try growing a little herb garden in a pot on the windowsill. Some of the best recipes take only a few good fresh ingredients to produce superior results. I wouldn't go hungry before I would use dried herbs, but I think you will notice a significant difference.

Don't garnish a plate with anything that doesn't look good enough to eat—no wilted parsley or soft strawberries.

KITCHEN TOOLS I FIND ESSENTIAL

- a good wire whisk

- a long-handled spoonula—which is a cross between a spoon and a spatula—made of spatula material but with a dished-out spoon on the end

- a set of good knives—buy one really good knife at a time if you can't spring for a whole set

- a thin, flexible cutting board

- a 2-quart glass mixing/measuring bowl—great for microwaving and for measuring larger amounts

- a really thin, flexible turner for pancakes or for removing cookies from cookie sheets

- a meat thermometer, digital if possible

- 2 sets of dry measuring cups— keeps you from having to stop and wash measuring cups during food preparation

- a short, fat spreader for spreading frosting or sandwich fillings

- a large mixing bowl, for whisking up those breakfast dishes

INDEX

ORDER AND RESERVATIONS

To order additional books email
barkley05@msn.com

1-800-888-1607. The Black Forest Inn is located 20 miles west of
Rapid City in the heart of the Black Hills.